Balkans 2010

*Report of an Independent Task Force
Sponsored by the
Council on Foreign Relations
Center for Preventive Action*

Edward C. Meyer, Chair
William L. Nash, Project Director

The Council on Foreign Relations is dedicated to increasing America's understanding of the world and contributing ideas to U.S. foreign policy. The Council accomplishes this mainly by promoting constructive debates and discussions, clarifying world issues, and publishing *Foreign Affairs*, the leading journal on global issues. The Council is host to the widest possible range of views, but an advocate of none, though its research fellows and Independent Task Forces do take policy positions.

THE COUNCIL TAKES NO INSTITUTIONAL POSITION ON POLICY ISSUES AND HAS NO AFFILIATION WITH THE U.S. GOVERNMENT. ALL STATEMENTS OF FACT AND EXPRESSIONS OF OPINION CONTAINED IN ALL ITS PUBLICATIONS ARE THE SOLE RESPONSIBILITY OF THE AUTHOR OR AUTHORS.

The Council will sponsor an Independent Task Force when (1) an issue of current and critical importance to U.S. foreign policy arises, and (2) it seems that a group diverse in backgrounds and perspectives may, nonetheless, be able to reach a meaningful consensus on a policy through private and nonpartisan deliberations. Typically, a Task Force meets between two and five times over a brief period to ensure the relevance of its work.

Upon reaching a conclusion, a Task Force issues a report, and the Council publishes its text and posts it on the Council website. Task Force reports can take three forms: (1) a strong and meaningful policy consensus, with Task Force members endorsing the general policy thrust and judgments reached by the group, though not necessarily every finding and recommendation; (2) a report stating the various policy positions, each as sharply and fairly as possible; or (3) a "Chairman's Report," where Task Force members who agree with the Chairman's report may associate themselves with it, while those who disagree may submit dissenting statements. Upon reaching a conclusion, a Task Force may also ask individuals who were not members of the Task Force to associate themselves with the Task Force report to enhance its impact. All Task Force reports "benchmark" their findings against current administration policy in order to make explicit areas of agreement and disagreement. The Task Force is solely responsible for its report. The Council takes no institutional position.

For further information about the Council or this Task Force, please write the Council on Foreign Relations, 58 East 68th Street, New York, NY 10021, or call the Director of Communications at (212) 434-9400. Visit our website at www.cfr.org.

CONTENTS

FOREWORD

The end of the Cold War enabled long-suppressed ethnic and religious conflicts to reemerge. Nowhere was the virus of militant ethnic nationalism more deadly than in the Balkans. Though too late to prevent the outbreak of violence in the former Yugoslavia, America and its allies ultimately played an indispensable role stopping atrocities, mediating agreements, and creating conditions for sustainable peace. After more than a decade of extensive involvement, the international community is looking to wind down its commitment in the Balkans.

The goal of the Council's Center for Preventive Action (CPA) is to develop and promote tangible, practical recommendations to avert deadly violence. Its Independent Task Force on the Balkans offers a systematic description of conditions required for the region to be on the path to integration with Europe and for the international community to reduce its presence in an orderly fashion by 2010. It identifies stakeholders and suggests ways to motivate key local actors as agents of conflict prevention. The Task Force is guided by the goal of changing how local leaders define their interests and convincing them to pursue policies and programs that would usher in a new era of peace and a better life for southeast Europe.

To this end, the Task Force report recommends specific milestones, benchmarks, and a timetable for action. It emphasizes measures to end ethnic violence, guarantee security for all communities, and allow persons displaced by conflict to return to their homes. It advocates continued international engagement, including the use of conditionality and "carrots and sticks," and recommends a shift in the priorities of the international community toward the standards and structures laid out in the European Union and NATO accession plans. It suggests strategies to achieve a sound institutional and legal basis for the development of free market economies and regional economic integration. The report also underscores the importance of cracking down on organized crime, which is eroding the rule of law throughout the region.

Today the mantle of leadership rests squarely on Europe's shoulders, and the Task Force is encouraged by the European Union's commitment to help the Balkan states move toward integration into European structures and standards. But this is not Europe's task alone. The United States also bears responsibility for making sure that violence does not recur. There is one simple lesson to be drawn from the international community's experience in the Balkans: while transatlantic cooperation is essential, America must share Europe's leadership mantle in certain areas to ensure that the conditions for a peaceful and prosperous future can be attained.

Ultimately the responsibility for achieving sustainable peace rests with the new generation of democratically elected leaders in the Balkans. The Independent Task Force on the Balkans hopes that its recommendations will strengthen common purpose among reform advocates and outside actors and help the states of the region become stable, prosperous partners of the international community.

There are many who deserve much thanks. First among them is General Edward C. Meyer, former U.S. Army chief of staff, for so skillfully chairing the Task Force. Everything he does turns into intelligent work. Thanks for overall leadership of the Center for Preventive Action, the umbrella organization for the Task Force, goes as always to General John W. Vessey, former chairman of the Joint Chiefs of Staff. General Vessey has been the chair of the center for some eight years now and honors us with his wisdom and humor. A good deal of the credit for the heavy lifting and strategizing for the Task Force report and for the center's work as a whole belongs to William L. Nash, the director of the center and a former U.S. Army major general. Bill has everything it takes to turn ideas into action. We are also most grateful to the Hewlett Foundation and Mr. Joachim Gfoeller Jr. for their generous support.

Leslie H. Gelb
President
Council on Foreign Relations

ACKNOWLEDGMENTS

The Balkans 2010 report is the product of the first Independent Task Force since the Center for Preventive Action was reestablished in 2001. This endeavor proved a worthy test of the center's mission and methodology. With this beginning, future task forces will continue to refine the process of identifying and targeting stakeholders and developing the "carrots and sticks" approach to conflict prevention.

The Balkans 2010 Task Force was fortunate in being ably led by a former chief of staff of the U.S. Army, General Edward C. Meyer. General Meyer's wisdom, experience, good humor, and ability to create concrete recommendations out of abstract discussions were crucial to this enterprise. It was great working for him again. All of the Task Force members and observers in New York and Washington, D.C., gave much of their time, knowledge, and judgment in pursuit of our endeavor. Thomas Lippman, a seasoned journalist, brought cohesion as well as readability to the written report. Colonel Robert L. McClure, U.S. Army, military fellow at the Council, planned and orchestrated a super fact-finding trip to the region. And most important, Kathleen M. Jennings, research associate at the center, was instrumental in keeping the project on track and on target. To all, my deepest appreciation.

Les Gelb's vision, drive, and insistence on high standards helped guide our work throughout and were crucial to our success. Jan Murray, Council senior vice president, worked closely with us to ensure that the job was done right. As always, the entire Council staff provided the support and advice we needed. It's a pleasure to work with such a great team.

The Hewlett Foundation and Council member Joachim Gfoeller Jr. provided not only crucial financial underpinning but encouragement every step of the way. All of us at the center deeply appreciate their very tangible support.

The work of the Task Force is not finished with the publication of this report. Just as the international community must remain engaged in the Balkans, so the Center for Preventive Action will continue the effort of forwarding and following up on the recommendations made here: writing opinion pieces, prompting congressional hearings, convening private meetings with the appropriate local and international stakeholders, and more. The key is to persevere, to convince those who can take action that the strategies offered by the center can work. We will continue to argue to leaders and citizens that conflict prevention in the Balkans and elsewhere can be an effective instrument of U.S. foreign policy.

William L. Nash
Council on Foreign Relations

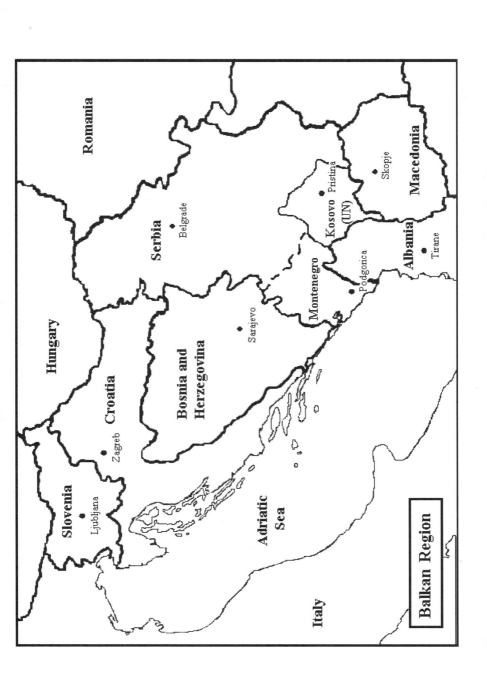

Balkan Region

Romania

Hungary

Slovenia

Ljubljana

Croatia

Zagreb

Serbia

Belgrade

Bosnia and
Herzegovina

Sarajevo

Kosovo
(UN)

Pristina

Montenegro

Podgorica

Macedonia

Skopje

Albania

Tirane

Adriatic
Sea

Italy

EXECUTIVE SUMMARY

For the states of the former Yugoslavia, the last decade was characterized by autocratic governance, armed conflict, and ethnic cleansing. Ever since the fighting ended, the international community and some local leaders have recognized that systemic political, economic, and social reforms are needed to build legitimacy, transparency, and the rule of law. But it hasn't happened yet.

The Center for Preventive Action, a project of the Council on Foreign Relations, designed the "Balkans 2010" Independent Task Force as an endeavor to prevent conflict by promoting tangible, practical recommendations for self-sustaining peace and development in the region.[1] The Task Force's mandate was threefold: to identify the key stakeholders—including governments, international organizations, nongovernmental organizations (NGOs), and the business and financial communities—in the Balkan region; to craft realistic, specific recommendations targeted at those stakeholders and at the political and economic leaders of the Balkan governments; and to take a "carrots and sticks" approach to conflict prevention and political development, paying particular attention to measures that strengthen those who pursue modernization and moderation while weakening those who espouse irredentism and stagnation.

The Task Force was convened before September 11, 2001, when the violence in Macedonia still received prominent international play as an early test of the then-new Bush administration, and when the fall of Serbian president Slobodan Milosevic was still recent enough to leave open the question of what international involvement would be appropriate and necessary in the newly democratic region as it struggled with its transition toward a broader European structure. After September 11, the international resources

---

[1] The particular areas covered in this report include Serbia and Montenegro, Bosnia and Herzegovina, Croatia, Macedonia, and the UN–administered Kosovo. Slovenia is not included in the report.

and attention shifted from the region—but the need for sustained commitment by the international community continues.

Accordingly, the Task Force has focused its recommendations on specific actions that will wisely use the resources that remain on the most important Western interests: preventing the region from becoming a vacuum in which organized crime and terrorism predominate and poverty fuels migration to Europe and America; and building partners in southeast Europe to help reach out to countries in Central Asia and the Middle East, where the challenges of the next generation will be felt. In effect, the Task Force proposes an agenda that, while not wholly new, acknowledges that the international community faces new challenges after September 11 and seeks to prepare the region to help in meeting those challenges.

The Task Force believes that outsiders can and should be encouraged to mobilize the political will and forge the specific policies and programs necessary to avert further deadly conflict and achieve a sustainable peace. In keeping with the Center for Preventive Action's founding mission, the Task Force's goal was to devise recommendations that provide realistic road maps for action and to formulate incentives that change how leaders define their interests, not to resort to a series of moralizing "oughts," "shoulds," and "musts."

The Balkan violence of the 1990s has run its course. With democratic governments in all of the former Yugoslav republics and region-wide ambitions to join the European Union (EU) and North Atlantic Treaty Organization (NATO), there is no longer a risk of major war between states. The Dayton Agreement ended the brutal war in Bosnia and Herzegovina (BiH) and continues to provide both a framework for that country to move toward Europe and the means to root out the ethnic separatism that still holds it back. In Kosovo, the repression of the ethnic Albanians has ended and work has begun to rebuild that damaged society. Slobodan Milosevic, the primary architect of the decade's violence, is on trial for his crimes at the international tribunal in The Hague. Across the states and regions of the former Yugoslavia, democratic governments share a common ambition to join the EU and NATO.

Nevertheless, sources of instability remain. Economic stagnation has generated unemployment and underemployment. Hundreds of thousands of refugees and displaced families still await return or resettlement. Money for reconstruction and development is inadequate. Prominent accused war criminals remain at large. Key institutions have resisted reform. Political and legal reform are impeded by corruption and by entrenched obstructionist forces—including organized crime syndicates—that rely on extremism and aggression to advance narrow, personal, or ethnically driven claims and grievances. Neglecting these challenges will have severe and destabilizing consequences for southeast Europe, including growing poverty; an increase in illegal economic activity, including trafficking in people and drugs; further human displacement; and a greater likelihood of political extremism, insurgency, and terrorism.

A renewal of conflict, however limited, would be devastating for the region and beyond. It would be an especially serious blow to Europe, raising the specter of increased refugee flows. But it would also have an impact on U.S. interests. Renewed conflict would be a policy failure with damaging implications for Balkan Muslims and for U.S. relations with the broader Muslim world. It would be an unwelcome diversion from other priorities; would increase the amount of drug and other trafficking that reaches Europe and beyond; and would enable terrorists to use the region as a transit hub or a haven.

Reversion to violence can be avoided through continued, albeit reconfigured and rebalanced, engagement by Europe and the United States. It is in the United States' and the EU's interests to provide the "carrots and sticks" that will keep Balkan governments on the path of progress and reform. These efforts will be more effective if the United States and the EU act in harmony. Failure to do so could result in a costlier and more dangerous intervention down the line and act as an unnecessary irritant in EU-U.S. relations.

The Task Force's overall vision for the Balkans centers on its integration into Europe—both formally, in terms of shared structures and institutions, and informally, in terms of shared norms and ideals. A coordinated international effort with shared objectives and clear lines of responsibility can, in cooperation with reform-oriented local leaders, put the Balkan states on the path to full integration with western Europe by 2010. Such an effort will encourage and assist a wide-ranging transformation of the political, economic, and legal systems in the region that will make it possible, over the next six to eight years, for the international community to reduce its presence in an orderly fashion and transfer responsibilities to capable indigenous actors and institutions.[2]

The main outside actors in the Balkan region are drawn from four groups: governments, supranational and international organizations, NGOs, and the commercial sector. From this assortment, certain key players—stakeholders—emerge. These stakeholders possess the political, economic, social, and military means to influence, cajole, or compel the Balkan governments to act in ways consistent with the development of democratic governance, market economies, civil societies, and ethnically integrated militaries under civilian democratic control. Among governments, the key stakeholders are the United States and certain member states of the EU, particularly Germany, Greece, Italy, the United Kingdom, and France. Among supranational and international organizations, the most important stakeholder in the Balkans is the EU, with NATO, the United Nations (UN), the World Bank, the International Monetary Fund (IMF), and, for the time being, the ad hoc civilian international operations in the region—chiefly the UN Mission in Kosovo (UNMIK) and the Office of the High Representative (OHR) in Bosnia and Herzegovina—playing significant roles. Within the nongovernmental sector, a considerable international presence comprised of Western grant-making foundations, advocacy groups, and service providers—such as the Soros foundations network, the International Crisis Group, the National Endowment for

---

[2] In terms of the security presence in the region, it should be noted that the Task Force believes that it is essential that NATO's military commitment to the Balkans continue, even if the size and nature—from security forces to security *development* forces—of NATO's presence change over time. This is important for psychological as well as deterrent reasons. For more on this argument, see Appendixes A-1 to A-3.

Democracy, and the International Rescue Committee—operate on the grassroots level to promote democracy, transparency, and civil society development, to train local partners, and to provide humanitarian relief. Finally, the business community in the Balkans, though nascent, is attracting European and American investors through the opening of markets and the widespread privatization of state-owned industries. This opening to business remains contingent upon the strengthening of property rights, reform of commercial laws and civil courts, and the region's overall stability.[3]

Europeans have the most direct and obvious interests in preventing further Balkan chaos: an economic interest in developing markets and trade routes with the region, and a security interest in protecting the frontier of the European Union against criminal activity, instability, and refugee flows. The EU is taking the lead in providing economic and technical assistance and encouraging political reform and stability in the Balkans, with the aim of elevating the Balkan states' standards of economic and political governance to EU norms. As the single largest assistance donor to the countries of the former Yugoslavia, with $4.65 billion committed from the European Commission budget for 2000–2006 (in addition to bilateral aid and the provision of peacekeeping troops from member states), the EU and its agencies—including the European Investment Bank (EIB) and the European Agency for Reconstruction (EAR)—will be at the core of reform and modernization efforts. The EU's Stabilization and Association Process (SAP) lays out actions required to join the union, with incentives for reform and disincentives for backsliding. This process is the fundamental road map for progress toward a closer association with Europe.

The United States is also a key stakeholder in the Balkans. The United States shares the EU's security concerns and has other longstanding interests in the region as well. Since 1945, American

---

[3] For an overview of international involvement in the region, and for information on the Balkan governments, see Appendix F.

administrations of both parties have accepted the premise that American security and economic interests require a peaceful and stable Europe. Continued U.S. engagement will reassure its partners of America's commitment to democracy and stability in the region and contribute to fulfillment of the vision of a "Europe whole and free." The new countries created from the former Yugoslavia are also strategically important as a bridge to current or aspirant EU and NATO members—Greece, Turkey, Bulgaria, and Romania—and to the Middle East. As noted above, abandoning the Muslim populations of Bosnia and Kosovo to face new threats from their neighbors will further reduce America's standing in the Muslim world and may encourage Balkan Muslims to turn to religious militants, rather than to Europe, for protection. Put simply, America's security will suffer if the Balkans slide toward division, lawlessness, and religious or ethnic conflict.

The U.S. interest is to support the Balkan states' efforts to reform—in particular using its influence in NATO to ensure a stable security situation and to guide military reform—while recognizing, and supporting, the European Union's lead role in providing political, economic, and technical assistance. Based on current spending patterns, the Task Force estimates that the United States will spend $8 billion to $12 billion on military operations and $2 billion to $3.5 billion on assistance to the Balkan region between now and 2010.[4] A continued U.S. commitment at this level is essential to the successful transformation of the region. Working together between now and 2010, the European Union and the United States can shepherd the Balkans along the path to full integration into Europe.[5]

---

[4] These estimates are based on an extrapolation of fiscal year (FY) 2003 figures. The military cost is based on a reduction of forces to between 4,000 and 6,000 U.S. soldiers in the region through 2010, with a faster draw-down depending on an improved security environment for minorities in Kosovo. It should be noted that some members of the Task Force believe that it is necessary for U.S. forces to remain at current levels in Bosnia and Kosovo, at least until the principal reforms outlined in the report have been successfully implemented and the threat from extremist elements has been eliminated. Currently the U.S. military provides approximately 15 percent of the forces in Bosnia and Kosovo.

[5] Though the United States continues to have the most influence of any foreign state in the Balkans, Germany, Italy, Greece, and the United Kingdom are also important players. Germany has committed a total of €614 million ($598 million) between 2000 and 2003

NATO's military commitment in the Balkans includes the Stabilization Force (SFOR) in Bosnia, the Kosovo Force (KFOR) in Kosovo, and Operation Amber Fox in Macedonia. It is important to recognize that approximately 85 percent of the forces in these NATO operations are non-U.S. forces. Beyond its peacekeeping responsibilities (which, in Bosnia, have included the capture of suspected war criminals), NATO is also involved in the region through its Partnership for Peace (PFP) program and Membership Action Plan (MAP). Taken together, these programs are the means by which Balkan countries can develop their own military and police forces, under democratic civilian control, that are professional and in the service of the state and its citizenry.

The World Bank disburses loans, grants, and technical and development assistance through its offices located in Albania, Bosnia and Herzegovina, Croatia, Macedonia, and Belgrade (for Serbia and Montenegro). A joint World Bank–European Commission Office on southeast Europe acts as a clearinghouse for donor countries and organizations; it coordinates aid projects in the region, provides needs assessments, devises strategies for regional development, and mobilizes support among donors. It does not disburse loans.

The carrots available to the Balkan governments from these stakeholders are abundant. As befits its primary role in the development of the region, the European Union has the most to offer. In return for continued peace, stability, and political and economic reform, the countries earn closer association with European institutions and structures, including privileged political and

---

for Stability Pact purposes and also disburses smaller amounts annually as part of its regular bilateral development cooperation with southeast Europe. Germany is also a main bilateral donor in Kosovo. Meanwhile, Italy has set aside approximately €196 million ($191 million) for bilateral initiatives and soft loans to Balkan countries for the years 2001–2003, in addition to its contributions to the EU aid budget. At the Federal Republic of Yugoslavia donors conference in June 2001, Italy pledged the most of any individual donor, committing over €115 million ($112 million) to Serbia and Montenegro's reconstruction. The United Kingdom contributes approximately 17 percent of all EU aid to the region. Finally, Greece is implementing a Hellenic Plan for Economic Reconstruction of the Balkans—separate from the EU aid policy to the region—with a provisional budget of €550 million ($536 million), and is also active in facilitating trade and investment incentives and infrastructure rehabilitation in the region.

economic relations and favorable trade terms on most goods. Both the European Union and the United States also offer economic, technical, and reconstruction assistance. Development assistance, largely in the form of loans, is also available from the World Bank. In the case of Serbia and Montenegro, the granting of normal trade relations is another carrot that the United States can offer in return for economic reform. Active involvement in NATO's PFP and MAP will enable states to reform and improve their militaries; develop interoperability with NATO; and prepare force structures, procedures, and capabilities for possible future membership.

The primary stick at the disposal of these stakeholders is conditionality—the linking of international assistance to specific performance goals. Conditionality is effective when the international community, especially the United States and the EU, speaks with one voice, because it puts pressure on local leaders to make difficult and unpopular changes and gives them political cover for doing so. It can be used to overcome popular and institutional resistance to the enactment of reform legislation for economic restructuring and privatization; to the elimination of discriminatory laws and practices; to the reform of the military, police, and judiciary; and to cooperation with the International Criminal Tribunal for the former Yugoslavia (ICTY).[6]

The Task Force recommends, however, that conditions be set in broad terms, with time limits sufficiently liberal to allow local actors some leeway in achieving the required standards. Inflexible and arbitrary cut-off dates can be counterproductive when substantial progress toward the required standards is underway. But when there is continuous failure to abide by conditions—for example, when corruption is massive and institutionalized, and no action is being taken to eradicate it—the international community must be willing to halt its funding to demonstrate the consequences of inaction.[7]

---

[6] Direct relief and support to refugees are not to be affected by conditionality regimes.

[7] The best example of the positive use of conditionality occurred with the transfer of Slobodan Milosevic to The Hague tribunal in 2001; strict enforcement by the United States of deadlines provided the Serbian government with the motivation to take action on time.

Two of the other major stakeholders in the region—UNMIK in Kosovo and the OHR in Bosnia—have different means of persuasion at their disposal. Both UNMIK and the OHR have direct policy responsibilities in their assigned areas. Kosovo is essentially a UN protectorate and UNMIK, in cooperation with the EU office in Kosovo and the Organization for Security and Cooperation in Europe (OSCE), continues to perform many of its basic administrative and governmental functions. The OHR, meanwhile, oversees the implementation of the civilian aspect of the Dayton Peace Agreement and can impose legislation and dismiss obstructive officials. The Task Force recommends that these ad hoc organizations be gradually phased out in favor of indigenous institutions and a smaller international presence, with the European Union taking the lead.[8] However, for the moment they are effective, if unrepresentative, tools for pushing through difficult or unpopular reforms in Kosovo, and especially in Bosnia.

External stakeholders are, obviously, only a part of the whole picture—the ultimate goal for the international community in the region is to turn over responsibility to local leaders who are accountable to their fellow citizens and who support democratic values. In this respect, the signs are somewhat encouraging. With Slobodan Milosevic and Croatian president Franjo Tudjman gone, for the first time all the states in the region are essentially democratic and committed to building market economies.

Nevertheless, there is still a risk of backsliding in the region: the security situation in Macedonia remains tenuous; the coalition government in Serbia is irretrievably splintered; and in Kosovo all the political parties are organized around ethnic objectives and pander to nationalist sentiment. In Bosnia and Herzegovina, meanwhile, the elections in October 2002—which resulted in presidential victories for the three main nationalist parties at the expense of their moderate competitors—demonstrate that nationalist feelings remain potent. One reason for these trends is the increasing discontent of local populations whose embrace of the West has failed to bring immediate improvements in their standard of liv-

---

[8] See Appendix A.

ing. Disturbingly, parties uninterested in bringing their countries closer to the European mainstream could benefit in elections over the next few years. The hard truth is that, while all the major parties in such states as Bulgaria and Romania—as in Poland, Hungary, and the Czech Republic earlier—have endorsed their countries' continued efforts to join the European Union and NATO, such an outcome is not preordained for the states of the former Yugoslavia, with the exception of Slovenia. Irredentist, criminal, and antidemocratic forces will try to exploit people's frustration brought on by the difficulties inherent in transitions, and it is these elements that must be countered through active engagement by the European Union, the United States, and the United Nations. These stakeholders, and the international community as a whole, need to make clear the economic, political, and security benefits of cooperation and reform, and they must also be equally explicit about the penalties—including the withholding of financial aid and international isolation—for regression, obstructionism, or the use of violence.

FINDINGS AND RECOMMENDATIONS

Setting the Balkans irreversibly on the path to EU standards of governance by 2010 requires a broad range of coordinated activities by the stakeholders in five key areas: 1) reevaluation and clarification of the objectives of the international community and reorganization of the structure of the international presence in the region; 2) establishment of the rule of law and development of systems of criminal and civil justice that are—and are perceived to be—fair and effective for all citizens; 3) restructuring of economies, including the banking, taxation, trade, and pension systems; 4) return or resettlement of refugees and internally displaced persons (IDPs) in a way that respects individual choice; and 5) education reform and establishment of a vigorous civil society, including a free and responsible press. Accomplishing these objectives will require the coordinated engagement of a cohesive international community, working in tandem with reformist local leaders.

In the Balkan region, a necessary first step is the recognition—by the political elite, military commanders, opinion makers, and, ultimately, the majority of the public—that their future lies in Europe, and that the path to closer European integration requires cooperation with other regional leaders and European officials and the implementation of difficult political and economic decisions. Those who abide by these principles are to be supported; those who do not are to be marginalized.

The cohesiveness of the international community is another key element if progress is to be made in the Balkans. The European Union's Stabilization and Association Process and NATO's Partnership for Peace program and Membership Action Plan are the planning blueprints around which the international community can most usefully prioritize and organize its activities, incentives, and penalties.[9] These programs, taken as a whole, provide

---

[9] For more information on the SAP and NATO programs, see Appendix A-1.

the necessary standards for association with, and integration into, Europe.[10]

To maximize the efficiency and cooperation of the two most influential stakeholders—the European Union and the United States—the Task Force recommends that the EU authorize the key officials responsible for the SAP to act as interlocutors with their U.S. counterparts, with a mandate to increase coordination on both long-term strategy and day-to-day activities. It also recommends that the United States designate a person or group, at the senior executive-branch level, authorized to act in coordination with the European Union and given interdepartmental assets and responsibilities that span the entire Balkan region. Within the U.S. government ranks, increasing the coordination between the staffs of the Department of State and the Department of Defense will improve the effectiveness of U.S. policy initiatives in the region. Such a reform would also serve as a model for better civil-military relations between other actors in the Balkans, particularly the European Union and NATO.

Setting priorities along the lines of the EU and NATO plans will require the reorganization, over time, of the international presence in the Balkans. This reorganization is overdue. Overlapping mandates, operational inefficiencies, and conflicting signals arising from a mélange of standing and ad hoc participants characterize the current organizational structure in the region. Streamlining and systematizing this presence, through the gradual phasing out of ad hoc civilian international operations such as the OHR in Bosnia, will provide the Balkan states with a consistent, clear set of priorities, standards, and requirements for progress on the path to Europe.

---

[10] As of August 2002, Croatia and Macedonia have signed Stabilization and Association Agreements (SAAs) with the EU. Since the death of Franjo Tudjman in 1999 and the election of a reformist government in 2000, Croatia has made significant progress in most reform areas, though improvement is still required with regard to refugee return. Croatia enjoys certain advantages over other Balkan countries, including a strong tourist industry and a more intact infrastructure. The fighting ended early in Croatia relative to elsewhere in the region; the international presence has never been as intrusive as in Bosnia and Kosovo; and NATO's involvement there has been minimal and centers around Croatia's participation in the Partnership for Peace. For these reasons, certain of the recommendations issued in this report do not pertain to Croatia.

It will also enhance the international community's ability to demand accountability from laggard governments and individual obstructionists.

Establishing the European Union and NATO plans as priorities in the Balkans, and reorganizing the international presence in the region to reflect that, are the first steps. Reforms are also essential in the areas of rule of law, economic restructuring, refugee policy, and civil society. As argued above, conditionality is an important, if not essential, tool of the international community in ensuring that these additional reforms are enacted in a timely manner.

Strengthening the rule of law is crucial for political and economic development, the protection of minority rights, and the maintenance of stable internal and regional security environments. Indeed, the rule of law is the foundation upon which reforms in other areas—the economy, refugee policy, civil society—will be built, and it must be accorded due importance by international policies and programs, especially the EU's Stabilization and Association Process.[11]

Among other things, building the rule of law requires local governments, with assistance from international police and NATO forces if necessary, to take the lead in arresting and extraditing war criminals. Other essential tasks for the Balkan governments include eliminating discriminatory provisions from all constitutions and statutes; removing individuals associated with violence or crime from positions of authority in national and municipal governments; and respecting and restoring property rights, particularly where refugees are concerned. Technical and financial aid from the European Union, the U.S. Agency for International Development (USAID), the OSCE, and others will be necessary to assist local authorities in drafting and enforcing legislation to fight corruption and organized crime, as well as in providing retraining programs and sufficient pay for law enforcement personnel, including judges and customs agents. It is also important that the international community of states and international and

---

[11] This issue is examined in greater detail in Appendix B.

nongovernmental organizations strengthen the authority and expand the resources of the International Criminal Tribunal for the former Yugoslavia so that proceedings against important fugitives (particularly Radovan Karadzic and Ratko Mladic) take place. The tribunal and local authorities can work together on remaining cases, with the aim of transferring them to local jurisdictions as soon as possible and allowing the tribunal to wrap up its work between 2007 and 2009.

Certain changes are clearly priorities for the economic teams of all the governments of the Balkan states. Reform of the banking sector is a critical first step in order to build a dynamic economy capable of providing employment, producing quality goods and services, and raising standards of living. Such reform requires the Balkan governments' economic teams to liquidate banks that are not viable and to rehabilitate and sell the remaining banks to better-capitalized foreign or domestic groups.[12] Accelerating the privatization and restructuring of state- or publicly owned corporations, and liberalizing trade and customs procedures consistent with EU standards, are also necessary steps. These reforms can be aided by EU-funded technical assistance programs. Enactment of each of these reforms will bring in much-needed foreign capital and expand opportunities for domestic investors.

Another key to increasing domestic and foreign investment is the development of the private sector. Local governments, with technical and financial assistance from the international financial institutions, can abet this process by establishing lending vehicles, especially to support small and medium-sized enterprises, and by promoting business training programs—which can themselves be devised and funded by nongovernmental organizations or grant-making foundations. Rebuilding physical infrastructure and establishing mortgage-finance systems, which help the labor pool become more mobile, also are key elements of an investment

---

[12] The process of liquidation or consolidation and rehabilitation is already underway throughout the region, particularly in Serbia and Bosnia. Moreover, foreign banks—especially those based in Germany, Austria, Greece, and Italy—are becoming an increasingly strong force in the region. See Appendix C.

promotion strategy. The former can be accomplished using funds and guarantees provided by foreign aid and local public financing; the latter function can be assumed by rehabilitated, privately owned savings banks, with government backing if necessary.

Refugee policy also requires revamping.[13] The High Commissioner for Refugees (UNHCR) is rightly the architect of the effort, but the dedicated energy and involvement of the European Union, the United States, and NATO are required. Nongovernmental organizations that provide job training, housing, and social services for refugees and internally displaced persons are also important tools of policy formation and implementation.

One necessary step is the establishment of a regionwide working group—under the auspices of the European Union but including representatives from all governments, UNHCR, NATO, country-specific civilian international operations, and major NGOs—to coordinate direct dialogue and establish regional standards on the issues of pensions, property rights, compensation, and citizenship. Property rights and citizenship are also important issues for national legislatures. Two priorities are the creation, by local authorities, of an acceptable legal framework and procedural mechanism for property restitution or compensation, and the adoption, by national legislatures, of laws recognizing dual citizenship for refugees from other Balkan jurisdictions who have resettled in that country. Continued funding for refugee return, and for employment and training schemes and housing for both returning and resettled refugees, is also imperative; the UNHCR and the European Union, along with other relief agencies and local governments, are the primary funding sources. A crucial point implicit in this recommendation is that resettlement may be preferable to return for some individuals and families. Acceptance of this option by governments (especially the U.S. government) and international organizations, and adjustment of refugee policy where appropriate, are critical for the successful integration or re-integration of refugees into their communities. The Task Force also emphasizes

---

[13] See Appendix D for more details.

the need for the NATO missions in Bosnia, Kosovo, and Macedonia to continue providing security assistance for refugees, particularly minority returnees. In Bosnia, for example, refugees are returning to their homes at a higher rate each year—approximately 92,000 returned in 2001. Without such assistance, returns will not continue.

To develop civil society, national legislatures must enact measures granting legal status to NGOs and nonprofit groups.[14] Once this legal status has been established, the crucial next step for legislatures is to modify tax regimes to give tax-exempt status to not-for-profit organizations and individual donors, so as to enable local NGOs to become financially self-sufficient. Without such actions, the growth of civic organizations will be stunted, and those NGOs that do exist locally will remain dependent on external contributions. Civil society development will also hinge on the continued involvement of international NGOs, democracy promotion organizations, individual donors, and government agencies such as USAID and the United Kingdom's Department for International Development. These organizations provide training programs, fund-raising instruction, aid, and in-kind assistance.

Revision of curricula in education is also necessary. This is ultimately a matter for national and municipal authorities, but nongovernmental organizations—such as the Open Society Institute, Croatia, and the Center for Democracy and Reconciliation in Southeast Europe—can play a constructive, advisory role.

A free press is fundamental to the development of a vigorous civil society. Development of journalism through training and assistance requires the involvement of international NGOs, media organizations, and media watchdogs. Privatization of state-run media organizations, adoption by journalists and editors of a voluntary code of conduct, and expansion of training and exchange programs for journalists in cooperation with European and American organizations will reinforce the independence, credibility, and professionalism of print and broadcast journalism across the region.

---

[14] For more details, see Appendix E.

Finally, assuming that the Serbia-Montenegro agreement of March 2002 (which provides for a referendum on independence by either Montenegro or Serbia by 2005) will resolve the political status of Montenegro, at least temporarily, it remains necessary to determine the political status of Kosovo. The uncertainty over Kosovo's legal status inhibits economic investment and stokes irredentist sentiment among some factions of both Serbs and Albanians. The Task Force recognizes the difficulty of determining Kosovo's status and takes no position on what the final status should be, provided that the solution is reached through negotiation and is acceptable to the citizenry.

While acknowledging the strong views in Kosovo on the issue of final status, the Task Force believes that the Provisional Institutions of Self-Government (PISG) need to demonstrate their ability to govern, especially in ways that guarantee the human rights of all citizens. At the same time, the resolution of status needs to be done peacefully and in a manner that contributes to long-term stability.[15]

The Task Force feels that the specifics set forth in UNMIK's "Standards before Status" initiative of May 2002 constitute a valuable starting point, and it further recommends that direct talks between Belgrade and the new government in Pristina be undertaken within the next year to address technical and procedural issues and to lay the groundwork for future political discussions.[16] Issues under discussion at the talks can include (but are not limited to) property rights, pensions, use and ownership of electrical and water resources, and travel procedures. Cooperation between Serb and Kosovo authorities on refugee and IDP issues is also required; the regionwide refugee working group (recommended above) is a forum in which this can occur.

---

[15] A number of Task Force members note that there is also legitimate concern that pro-reform forces in Serbia would be undermined, perhaps fatally, by a move to resolve Kosovo's status at the present time—thus hobbling the very forces that the international community needs to nurture, and opening the door for anti-reform forces in Serbia to regain power.

[16] See Appendix A-3.

Regardless of timing, the Kosovo question is not to be linked in any way to the future of Republika Srpska, the Serb entity in Bosnia. The Task Force strongly believes that Republika Srpska as envisioned in the Dayton Peace Agreement should remain part of Bosnia and Herzegovina. The notion espoused by some Serbs that Republika Srpska be Serbia's "compensation" for the loss of Kosovo is inherently destabilizing and therefore unacceptable.

The case for international engagement in the Balkans cannot be examined as though the involvement were starting today. After the events of the past decade, the Balkans have become a test of European and American partnership and commitment. The United States and the European Union have invested immense resources in the region. Since the Task Force began its work in August 2001, the United States and its partners have taken on new commitments elsewhere in the world. In the Balkans, those with antidemocratic values are watching to see whether the United States and its partners have the staying power to finish the job they took on.

Finally, helping the Balkan countries engineer a successful future requires a unique combination of urgency and patience: urgency, because problems such as organized crime and impoverished refugees present a constant threat of instability; patience, because there are no overnight solutions and because, to maintain public support, these fragile democracies may have to proceed cautiously on occasion. Finding the right balance and acting upon it will be difficult and at times frustrating, but the potential reward—a Balkan region taking its place at last among the prosperous, democratic societies of a peaceful Europe—more than justifies the effort.

TASK FORCE MEMBERS

EDWARD C. MEYER, General, USA (Ret.), Chairman of the Balkans 2010 Independent Task Force, served as Chief of Staff of the United States Army from 1979 to 1983. He is Chairman Emeritus of Mitretek Systems, President of Army Emergency Relief, and Chairman of the George Marshall Foundation. General Meyer is also a Partner of Cilluffo Associates, a member of the Board of Trustees of the Smith Richardson Foundation, and a member of the Board of Overseers of the Hoover Institution.

KENNETH H. BACON is the President of Refugees International. Between 1994 and 2001, he served as the Assistant Secretary of Defense for Public Affairs and Pentagon spokesman.

GEORGE C. BIDDLE is the Senior Vice President of the International Rescue Committee. Previously, he was Vice President of the International Crisis Group and President of the Institute for Central American Studies.

ALEXANDER BORAINE is the founding President of the International Center for Transitional Justice, an Adjunct Professor at New York University, and the author, most recently, of *A Country Unmasked* (2000). From 1995 to 1998, he was the Deputy Chair of the South African Truth and Reconciliation Commission, serving under chairman Archbishop Desmond Tutu.

HANI K. FINDAKLY is CEO of Potomac Capital Inc. From 1986 to 2000, he held a number of senior investment banking and investment management positions on Wall Street. From 1975 to 1986 he served at the World Bank, where he was Director of Investments and Chief Investment Officer; before joining the bank, Dr. Findakly served on the faculty of MIT.

JOHN G. HEIMANN is Senior Adviser to both Merrill Lynch & Co., Inc., and the Financial Stability Institute of the Bank for International Settlements. He also acts as Senior Adviser to the Board of Directors of Allied Irish Bank. He served as New York State's Superintendent of Banks, U.S. Comptroller of the Currency, and a Member of the Board of both the Federal Deposit Insurance Corporation and the Federal National Mortgage Association.

JONATHAN E. LEVITSKY is an attorney with the law firm of Debevoise & Plimpton in New York. He previously served as Counselor to Ambassador Richard C. Holbrooke at the U.S. Mission to the UN, as a member of the State Department's Policy Planning Staff, and as a law clerk to U.S. Supreme Court justice John Paul Stevens.

THOMAS LIPPMAN is a former diplomatic correspondent of the *Washington Post* and was the *Post's* principal reporter during the NATO bombing campaign against Serbia in 1999. He is the author of *Understanding Islam* and of *Madeleine Albright and the New American Diplomacy.*

ROBERT L. MCCLURE is a Colonel in the U.S. Army and was the 2001–2002 U.S. Army Military Fellow at the Council on Foreign Relations.

MARGARET F. MUDD is Senior Adviser at the Financial Services Volunteer Corps, a nongovernmental organization. Formerly, she was a banker with long experience providing financial services to banks in the Balkans and in Eastern Europe.

WILLIAM L. NASH is a Senior Fellow and Director of the Center for Preventive Action at the Council on Foreign Relations.

JAMES C. O'BRIEN is a principal of the Albright Group, LLC, and served as special presidential envoy for the Balkans and Senior Adviser to Secretary of State Madeleine Albright during the Clinton administration. He participated in numerous high-profile international negotiations, including a leading role in the Dayton Peace Agreement in Bosnia.

SADAKO OGATA, former United Nations High Commissioner for Refugees, serves as Co-Chair of the Commission on Human Security and as Japanese prime minister Junichiro Koizumi's Special Representative for Afghanistan, and is Scholar-in-Residence at the Ford Foundation.

DAVID L. PHILLIPS is a Senior Fellow and Deputy Director of the Center for Preventive Action at the Council on Foreign Relations and has served as a Senior Adviser to the U.S. Department of State and the United Nations.

COLETTE RAUSCH specializes in rule of law issues in peace operations at the United States Institute of Peace. Before joining the institute, she was with the Organization for Security and Cooperation in Europe in Kosovo, serving as the Director of the Department of Human Rights and Rule of Law.

STEPHEN SAIDEMAN is an Associate Professor of Political Science at McGill University. His research largely focuses on the international and domestic politics of ethnic conflict, as does his recent book, *The Ties That Divide: Ethnic Politics, Foreign Policy, and International Conflict*.

MARK SCHNEIDER is the Senior Vice President of the International Crisis Group. Previously he served as Director of the Peace Corps. He has held senior positions at the U.S. Agency for International Development and at the Pan American Health Organization, a regional office of the World Health Organization.

DOUGLAS E. SCHOEN is a founding Partner and a Principal Strategist at the market research firm Penn, Schoen & Berland Associates. He has provided strategic advice to political candidates in the United States and to leaders around the world, including heads of state of Greece, Turkey, Israel, the Philippines, the Dominican Republic, Bermuda, and Yugoslavia.

DANIEL SERWER is the Director of the Balkans Initiative at the United States Institute of Peace, where he has worked extensively on democratization in Serbia and has been deeply engaged in facilitating dialogue between Serbs and Albanians. He served from 1994 to 1996 as U.S. Special Envoy and Coordinator for the Bosnian Federation, mediating between Croats and Bosniaks and negotiating the first agreement reached at the Dayton peace talks.

LAURA SILBER, Senior Policy Adviser at the Open Society Institute, plays a leading role in the institute's policy advocacy, part of which includes supervising efforts to promote the Open Society's policies and issues internationally through the media. From 1990 to 1997 she was the *Financial Times* Balkans correspondent, and she is the co-author of the critically acclaimed *Yugoslavia: Death of a Nation.*

PAUL WILLIAMS is the Rebecca Grazier Professor of Law and International Relations at American University and directs the Public International Law and Policy Group, which provides pro bono legal assistance to states in transition. He has previously served in the Department of State's Office of the Legal Adviser, as a Senior Associate at the Carnegie Endowment for International Peace, and as legal counsel to various parties during the Dayton, Rambouillet, Lake Ohrid, Key West, and Belgrade/Podgorica negotiations.

TASK FORCE OBSERVERS

GUILLERMO CHRISTENSEN was the 2001–2002 Intelligence Fellow at the Council on Foreign Relations.

JONATHAN DAVIDSON is Senior Adviser for Political and Academic Affairs at the European Commission Delegation in Washington, D.C., and an Adjunct Professor at Johns Hopkins University and American University. He served in the British Diplomatic Service from 1963 to 1981 in London, India, Thailand, Senegal, and the United States.

ARTHUR C. HELTON is Senior Fellow for Refugee Studies and Preventive Action at the Council on Foreign Relations. He is an expert on international refugee law and policy and is the author, most recently, of *The Price of Indifference: Refugees and Humanitarian Action in the New Century* (2002).

KATHLEEN M. JENNINGS is a Research Associate at the Center for Preventive Action at the Council on Foreign Relations.

JANICE L. MURRAY is Senior Vice President and Treasurer of the Council on Foreign Relations.

JULIA VADALA TAFT, a leading authority on refugee and humanitarian assistance, is currently the Assistant Administrator of the United Nations Development Programme and Director of the Bureau for Crisis Prevention and Recovery. Previously she served as Assistant Secretary of State for Population, Refugees, and Migration.

APPENDIXES

APPENDIX A: INTERNATIONAL PRESENCE, STRUCTURE, AND OBJECTIVES

I. OBJECTIVES OF THE INTERNATIONAL COMMUNITY

Achieving the goal of putting the Balkans on a path to stability and integration with Europe by 2010 will require sustained assistance, organized around three guiding principles:

—Keeping a robust international presence, led by the European Union and including an American component through 2010.

—Ensuring that the European Union (EU) and NATO are the primary agents of international influence in the Balkans over the coming decade. Ad hoc arrangements such as the Office of the High Representative in Bosnia, UN missions, and the Stability Pact can be phased out as the EU process becomes firmly established and as responsibilities are transferred to EU officials or, preferably, capable local leaders.

—Assumption by the people of the Balkans and their leaders of responsibility for their future. They cannot build stable democracies and thriving economies as passive recipients of aid and guidance from the international community.

Yet this does not translate into a "hands-off" approach for the international community. Instead, the international community's proper role is to support, and cooperate and coordinate with, reformist local leaders; to make this support tangible through political, economic, and technical assistance; and to make it clear that the continuation of this assistance is, to a large extent, dependent on the choices that the leaders and their people make, all the while emphasizing the financial and other benefits of sustained reform and normalization.[17]

These principles acknowledge the tacit bargain that was struck after the wars of Yugoslav disintegration and the fall of the Tudj-

---

[17] It should be stressed that security assistance, such as NATO missions and international policing, is not subject to conditionality, nor is direct relief to refugees and the internally displaced.

man and Milosevic regimes. All Balkan states have committed themselves to meeting contemporary European norms. In return, Europe's political, economic, and security institutions have agreed to facilitate the integration of the Balkan countries.

The European Union, the major stakeholder in the region, has articulated a vision for the Balkans: by 2010 it will be a region of stable, self-sufficient democracies, at peace with themselves and each other, with market economies and the rule of law, and which will be either members of the European Union or on the road to membership. The EU's Stabilization and Association Process (SAP) is the mechanism for reaching this goal.[18] The SAP establishes relationships between the European Union and the countries of the western Balkans, in which the European Union helps the countries prepare themselves for membership by rising to EU standards of governance. This process includes the Stabilization and Association Agreements (SAAs), which establish a contractual relationship between the signatory countries and the European Union and which represent the signatories' commitment to complete a formal association with the European Union. The process of preparing for, negotiating, and implementing an agreement itself constitutes an engine for change, with benchmarks of progress. In exchange for EU assistance, countries are required to demonstrate that they share the EU's core political values, including respect for human rights, regional cooperation, equitable solutions for refugees and the displaced, and full cooperation with the International Criminal Tribunal for the Former Yugoslavia (ICTY). They are also required to build market economies and administrations that can manage the levels of legal and economic integration that come with EU membership.

The main question for the United States is whether the European Union has the staying power and political will to see its strategy through. The Task Force recognizes that the European Union has assigned itself an unprecedented role in the Balkans. It is strongly in the U.S. interest to help the European Union stay the course, and to keep the EU accountable for its end of the deal. At the same

---

[18] See Appendix A-1.

time, the United States has unique capabilities that are unmatched by Europe but still needed in the Balkans: for example, the U.S. military is an essential deterrent to violence, and the United States is able to deploy additional force quickly if needed. The Task Force therefore believes that, for the next six to eight years, an active U.S. presence in the region will remain necessary.

NATO is also a crucial stakeholder in the Balkans, and its continued engagement is imperative. Simply put, NATO missions in Bosnia, Kosovo, and Macedonia cannot be discontinued until effective alternative public security forces have been developed. That being so, the formulation—by NATO and the Supreme Allied Commander, Europe (SACEUR)—of a long-term strategy in the Balkans, above and beyond the situation-specific deployments in Bosnia, Kosovo, and Macedonia, will enhance the security situation in the entire region. The underlying goal for this strategy is the development of security capacity, under civilian democratic control, in each Balkan country and the eventual transition of NATO units' role in individual areas from security forces to security *development* forces. The Membership Action Plan (MAP), Partnership for Peace (PFP) program, and joint military exercises are the basis for this strategy.

Thus the task force identifies three priorities for the international community:

—The establishment of the European Union's Stabilization and Association Process and NATO's Membership Action Plan and Partnership for Peace program as the basic road maps for the region's evolution, and the subsequent rationalization of the international presence according to the requirements and priorities expressed in those blueprints.

—The implementation of internationally led campaigns, initially in Bosnia and Kosovo, to cripple the politico-criminal syndicates that threaten internal and regional security.

—Restructuring of the international presence to eliminate independent policymaking by ad hoc structures—particularly in Bosnia and Kosovo—and the concomitant transfer of responsibilities to permanent European or local institutions.

The second priority will be examined first.

II. ATTACKING POLITICO-CRIMINAL SYNDICATES

In every Balkan state, there are people with the motivation and resources to subvert the movement toward moderation and integration into Europe. These subversive groups severely hinder local reformers' efforts to modernize and clean up their governments and economies. As politico-criminal syndicates—often fortified by riches from pirate privatization and bolstered by illegal connections across borders—their profits and survival depend on their stifling of efforts to introduce transparency and accountability into the political and economic systems of the state. Moreover, their combination of influence, access, resources, and superficially appealing ideology makes it difficult for relatively new governments to mount sustained campaigns against them. A vigorous international presence is essential to confront these politico-criminal groups until the Balkan governments have the capacity and will to do it themselves. Such campaigns can initially be launched in Bosnia and Kosovo, where the extent and authority of the international institutions are greatest. Those campaigns can then be emulated in Serbia and Montenegro, Macedonia, and Croatia, with the degree of international involvement varying according to the specific needs and preferences of local authorities.

Thwarting these politico-criminal syndicates will require a considerable infusion of expertise, resources, and muscle from the West. In Bosnia especially, progress in moving the country toward European standards of governance has been made only when the international community has confronted the syndicates' power over industry, government finances, borders, or the media.[19] Likewise, arrests of ethnic extremists, seizure of weapons, control of border crossings, travel and financial restrictions on key leaders, and improved law enforcement and intelligence cooperation played important roles in reducing ethnic violence in Kosovo, in southern

---

[19] Examples include the 1997 removal of media in Republika Srpska from nationalist control; the seizure in 2001 of a bank controlled by hard-line Croats, who had stolen from their own people; and the March 2002 decision by the OHR to remove constitutional provisions that helped nationalist parties retain control of public institutions and resources.

Serbia, and in Macedonia. While these efforts have been limited and pursued with insufficient vigor, the underlying lesson is clear:
*decisive actions aimed at the levers of power controlled by these
politico-criminal syndicates produce results.*

The Task Force therefore recommends that the Office of High
Representative (OHR) in Bosnia and the head of UN Mission in
Kosovo (UNMIK) Pillar I (which deals with police and justice issues)
in Kosovo set as a top priority the seizing of criminal institutions
and the pursuit, prosecution, and removal from office of individuals associated with illegal intersections of government and financial power. This activity can be initiated throughout the region no
later than the end of 2003 and is to be continued on the part of
the international community until local institutions acquire the ability and the will to take it upon themselves. Aid from the European Union and other donors can be conditioned on the removal
from authority of individuals associated with past crimes and
violence. Aid can also provide incentives for government officials
to cooperate with international initiatives. These conditionalities
can also compel neighboring countries to launch similar campaigns,
with varying degrees of international assistance and involvement.

III. RESTRUCTURING THE INTERNATIONAL PRESENCE

While a continued international presence in the Balkans is imperative, the current structure of international involvement in the Balkans is poorly organized, even counterproductive. The many
stakeholders (discussed in the Executive Summary) are often at
odds with each other. There is no coherent, consistent strategy.
Throughout the Balkans, ad hoc structures (the OHR, various UN
missions), regional missions (of the Organization for Security and
Cooperation in Europe [OSCE] or NATO), and pillars of the
post–World War II international framework (the World Bank, the
European Union) work independently, with coordination that ranges
from close to nonexistent. Although this morass of uncoordinated agencies was perhaps inevitable—given that the international presence in each country was created at different times, by

different organizations, under different circumstances—it has prevented international organizations from mounting concerted campaigns against the core elements that inhibit progress.

Indeed, it is increasingly obvious that the ad hoc nature of the international presence is an impediment to effective action on the most pressing issues. The makeshift structure puts an extra layer between the Balkan states and the institutions to which they aspire. This arrangement inhibits the effectiveness of the international agencies on the ground; confuses local actors when the signals coming from the various international agencies and institutions are competing or unclear; and may become a source of resentment for states anxious to demonstrate to their people that, after several years of hard choices, they are full partners in the main pillars of Europe. If this confusion and resentment continue to grow, the international presence will become less effective over time—just when the states of the region will have to tackle some of the most difficult issues impeding their integration into Europe. Thus, it is time to reduce the number of international officials and organizations able to set priorities and make decisions.

In any rational reconfiguration of the international presence in the Balkans, the European Union and NATO will take priority. The Balkan states' aim is to establish closer ties with the mainstream pillars of post–World War II Europe: these institutions provide the best rationale and the best political cover for local leaders to use in making difficult decisions and also provide the best leverage for the international community to use in promoting the required political, economic, and social changes to the Balkan states. Therefore, the international presence can be reorganized most effectively around the EU's accession process and NATO's Membership Action Plan and Partnership for Peace program. This will require streamlining the international structure in the region and systematizing it according to the priorities and standards established in the SAP and NATO projects. In conjunction with this reorganization, the United States needs to encourage Balkan countries that have not yet signed an SAA to meet the conditions for doing so within two years.

The international organizations also need to find opportunities to engage local opinion leaders, not simply elected or designated representatives of political parties. The Balkan region is in the midst of a remarkable and bumpy transition to democracy: from socialism to (in some places) war and post-conflict international governance, to self-government and alignment with EU norms. Encouraging local engagement in political decision-making and in the evolution of the international structures in the region is therefore critical to establish a feeling of ownership of the process among the local citizenry. If it is to be successful the process of Europeanization cannot occur just among elites; mass involvement is crucial. Local outreach by international organizations can take the form of town hall–style meetings to inform residents of, and receive feedback about, the tasks, tools, and goals of the international operation in their country; the use of local-language pamphlets, mailings, billboards, and websites to disseminate information; and cooperation with responsible local media.[20]

The overall goal for the international presence in the region is to eventually dismantle the ad hoc elements of the international presence and transfer that authority to permanent institutions like the European Union or, preferably, competent indigenous institutions. The European Union, NATO, and the UN can begin this restructuring process by 2004, with such matters to be deferred in Kosovo pending consideration of status issues.

To ease this transition process, the international organizations and operations need to prepare and publicize—through local media and the use of local-language pamphlets, public meetings, and governmental websites—their transition plans. These plans must identify the local governmental offices, or the ministries, that will assume responsibility for specific issues and tasks; detail how the transition will occur, and within what time frame; and identify a follow-up plan, specifying which offices or agencies within the European Union and NATO structures will retain responsibility for coordination, with local actors, on the major tasks required by the SAP and MAP/PFP after the transition period is complete. Requiring transition plans that are specific and publicizing them will allow the ad hoc organizations to explain how they are working with local governments, courts, police, and other authorities to prepare for the handover; highlight the local institutions that will be created or revamped to handle the increased responsibilities; and provide a strategy for the creation or rehabilitation of those institutions. Similarly, publicizing the follow-up plan will ensure that restructuring the international presence does not diminish accountability or action on the part of both the local and the international actors.

Until the handoff of responsibilities from ad hoc to permanent or indigenous institutions, however, there remains a pressing need for the reorganization of the intermediate agencies on the ground. Revision of the duties and authority of the OHR in Bosnia and Herzegovina is particularly pressing.

The OHR sits atop a huge, neo-colonial international structure but lacks clear decision-making authority over much of the international presence.[21] Civilian authority in Bosnia is continually renegotiated among major donors, impeding decisive action.

Giving the OHR in Bosnia the authority to establish priorities and set direction for all intergovernmental and international organizations working in the country—on the pillar model used by UNMIK in Kosovo—will strengthen that office and allow for clear decision-making until the restructuring of the international presence in Bosnia is complete. The Task Force was encouraged by recent efforts to strengthen the OHR's authority over the international organizations in Bosnia, including making the OHR the head of the EU mission as well.

The OHR's effectiveness will be improved by granting it executive authority over a small, armed law enforcement organization,

---

[21] The components of that presence include the United Nations, which advises and monitors domestic law enforcement and the judiciary but has authority to act only when local officials refuse to do so—and then lacks capacity; the OSCE, which enforces election requirements and investigates related financial fraud but does not have a mandate broad enough to confront nationalist agencies; and the autonomous NATO-led military presence, which, because it has a monopoly on the use of force on behalf of the international community, is often called upon to perform important law enforcement functions that are not part of its primary mission. All of these bodies report to shifting coalitions of states, which have their own evolving and often inconsistent political aims.

whose personnel are to be recruited by the European Union, with a mandate to conduct investigations, control crowds, and provide security as needed. The investigative expertise of such a unit would be critical, as would its ability to operate collectively (unlike groups of individual police trainers), especially in situations calling for crowd control or other unit maneuvers. This organization could also be the chief component of any action to dismantle the politico-criminal syndicates in Bosnia.

An armed police presence answerable to international *civilian* authorities might be controversial: since the Dayton Peace Agreement was signed, NATO has properly insisted on having a monopoly on the legitimate use of force in Bosnia. But continued dependence on the Stabilization Force (SFOR) in Bosnia and Herzegovina to fulfill policing functions is no longer workable. The absence of effective civilian law enforcement increases demands on the military. Simply put, is time for the U.S. government and NATO to acknowledge that it is not defensible to complain that military units are being asked to take on law enforcement responsibilities while at the same time refusing to endorse the establishment of an effective, armed law enforcement organization. Bosnia will make a constructive first assignment for the civilian police force that is to be created as part of the EU's rapid response initiative, provided it reports to the OHR.

IV. THE ROLE OF THE UNITED STATES

Notwithstanding the lead role of the European Union in shaping the future of the Balkans, there is a strong case for continued American engagement. It is based partly on the U.S. interest in the continuing project of building a free and undivided Europe, and partly on the need for U.S. power to confront the security threats posed by a vacuum of authority in the region.

It is important to achieve European-American agreement on the basic architecture of the Balkans—especially keeping current borders and boundaries unchanged unless all parties concerned agree.[22] In order to achieve effective day-to-day liaison and policy coordination, the Task Force recommends that the EU identify the officials responsible for the SAP (tracking progress, ensuring international support for the SAP requirements, and deciding upon the allocation of European assistance) and grant them authority to speak for the European Commission in discussions with a counterpart person or group designated by the United States.

A Europe whole and free has been a bipartisan American objective since the end of World War II. Indeed, the need for a solid relationship with a stable Europe has been a core premise of U.S. foreign policy for two generations. Premature U.S. disengagement from the Balkans will undermine this longstanding American policy. Even premature discussion of a U.S. withdrawal is counterproductive because it encourages malign groups in the Balkans that believe they can wait out the pressure to reform and, in due course, revert to their old ways.

The security threat—to the region, to western Europe, and to the United States—that would be created by neglect of the Balkans also argues for continued engagement. The problems associated with weak or failed states—such as political extremism, insurgency, lax border controls, terrorism, and other criminal activities including arms trafficking—are potentially destabilizing to the entire region and, by extension, to its European neighbors.

The exact nature of American involvement will change with the situation, but there are elements of American leadership that will always be crucial. One is the unique political weight of the United States. The European Union, for all the capabilities of its international representatives such as Christopher Patten and Javier Solana, still lacks the political coherence, cohesiveness, and power possessed by the United States. The authority the European Union has granted to Solana and Patten to speak on behalf of the EU, to offer political advice to Balkan governments, and to disburse aid is not matched by authority for other EU officials

---

[22] This does not preclude changes in political status, which remain an issue for Kosovo and, possibly, Montenegro.

to speak, nor are officials' words and actions fully coordinated. Each of the EU's fifteen member states, for example, retains sovereign powers to pursue separate policies and run uncoordinated aid programs abroad, notwithstanding efforts to forge a Common Foreign and Security Policy. The United States, on the other hand, has a single executive with authority to speak with one voice. In crisis situations, this authority is crucial and often determinative.

Additionally, certain issues—such as the final status of Kosovo, the transfer of indictees to The Hague, and security sector reform in Serbia—require U.S. political and diplomatic engagement. The United States also has a strong interest in continuing to support judicial reform, political party development, and NGO activism through its aid programs. Unique U.S. experience and clout add value to EU efforts in these important fields.

Above all, in the fragile security situation that still prevails— notably in Bosnia, Kosovo, and Macedonia—there is no credible alternative to U.S. military power, whether exercised unilaterally or through U.S. leadership of NATO, to deter insurgencies and restore peace as and when new crises flare up. The European Union's nascent effort to build a rapid reaction force may help in limited circumstances, but for the foreseeable future this will not replace the capacity of the United States and NATO to assure basic security in the most fragile states and entities of the region. Experience over the last decade has shown that U.S. political, diplomatic, and military presence is indispensable to ensure security and maintain stability in the Balkans, and that EU efforts are most effective when closely coordinated with and supported by the United States. While the EU is expected to assume an increasing share of the burden between now and 2010, it cannot undertake this task alone, and its own efforts to project security and stability will be far more effective with a continued U.S. presence on the ground, albeit at reduced levels.

V. THE UNITED STATES AND NATO

The strongest American presence in the Balkans is through NATO. Indeed, NATO's North Atlantic Council (NAC) and

SACEUR are the means through which the United States can most productively exercise its influence on a daily basis. It would be dangerous for NATO to withdraw at this stage, and as long as NATO is committed, the United States is committed.

NATO's missions in the region have drawn down steadily since the end of the conflicts in Bosnia and Kosovo. In Bosnia, force levels have fallen from more than 60,000 troops in 1996 to fewer than 15,000 in 2002. The United States now contributes fewer than 3,000 soldiers. The Kosovo Force (KFOR) has shrunk from almost 50,000 troops to approximately 36,000. Less than 5,000 of these are provided by the United States. The mission of NATO in Kosovo is twofold: to deter the renewal of inter-ethnic violence, both within Kosovo and on the border with Macedonia; and to provide political reassurance that the West is committed to the security and autonomy of Kosovo (without pre-judging its final status), and to the safety of minorities within Kosovo. NATO also operates a much smaller mission—Operation Amber Fox—in Macedonia.

It is imperative that NATO's missions in the region continue. In Kosovo and Macedonia, the objectives of the forces remain pressing. In Bosnia, the authority of the NATO mission is broadly written, in the expectation that NATO will engage in tasks beyond the strictly military and preserve its monopoly on the use of force. But those broader tasks are not being routinely performed, and no alternative has been created.

Over time, active participation in NATO's Membership Action Plan and Partnership for Peace program will bring the region's militaries under democratic civilian control, with the capacity and willingness to become self-sustaining stability forces for the protection of *all* their citizens. As part of these programs, countries are required to modernize their armed forces and reduce the number of military personnel to reflect their actual missions. Toward this end, a priority for NATO is to work with authorities in Bosnia to restructure and eliminate its multiple militaries. It is appropriate that Bosnia have one army or none—it neither needs, nor can it afford, three. As indigenous capacity is developed in Bosnia and throughout the region, NATO's presence on the ground will evolve into an advisory role.

Already NATO is engaged in an extensive program of exercises and training in the region. Even in Serbia, target of the NATO bombing campaign in 1999, prominent civilian officials espouse participation in the Partnership for Peace program—which contributes to democratization and civilian control of the military—as a first step toward integration with Western security institutions. Permanent basing of NATO forces throughout the region, or at least the designation of some sites as NATO training facilities, will establish a NATO presence beyond the current missions in Bosnia, Kosovo, and Macedonia.

VI. RUSSIA IN THE BALKANS

Any discussion of the international role in the Balkans would be incomplete without considering the interests of Russia, which for hundreds of years has seen itself as an important player in the region. Russia has become a defender of the region's Orthodox populations, but it could build deeper connections to the citizens rather than simply to the governments. However, most of the Balkan states are now looking westward toward a European future, as is Russia. The Task Force believes this issue needs to be discussed openly with the Russians—not to offer them a veto over the desires of the region's people, but to make this process part of Russia's own opening to the West. Russia has so far acquiesced in NATO's expansion, and even played an active, constructive role by participating in NATO-led missions, but in the Balkans the relationship could be nurtured into more than acquiescence. Indeed, the region has become a laboratory for cooperation between Russia and the United States and its partners. In this regard, the new relationship between Russia and NATO offers even greater possibilities.

A-1: SUMMARY—STABILIZATION AND ASSOCIATION
PROCESS, MEMBERSHIP ACTION PLAN, AND PARTNERSHIP
FOR PEACE PROGRAM

The Task Force's vision for the Balkans centers around the region's integration into European structures and institutions. The European Union's Stabilization and Association Process and NATO's Membership Action Plan and Partnership for Peace program provide the blueprint for the achievement of this vision. Taken as a whole, these programs supply the necessary standards and benchmarks for association with, and integration into, Europe. The following briefs provide descriptions of the major aspects of the SAP, MAP, and the PFP.

I. THE EUROPEAN UNION'S STABILIZATION
AND ASSOCIATION PROCESS

The European Union's Stabilization and Association process was initiated in 1999 and formally launched at the Zagreb summit on November 24, 2000. It represents a long-term commitment by the European Union of political, financial, and human resources for the development of the Balkan region. The SAP combines the development of privileged political and economic relations between the European Union and the Balkans with a substantial financial assistance program called CARDS (Community Assistance for Reconstruction, Development, and Stabilization).

The cornerstone of the SAP is the Stabilization and Association Agreement, which establishes a contractual relationship between the signatory country and the European Union. The conclusion of an SAA represents the signatory's commitment to complete, over a transition period, a formal association with the European Union. This association is based on the implementation over time of core obligations, including the establishment of a free trade area; the enactment of political, economic, and other reforms necessary to achieve EU standards; and the harmonization of domestic legislation with that of the European Commission, especially on economic matters. Once countries have signed an SAA, the European Union can use the mechanisms entailed by the agreement to help them prioritize reforms, shape those reforms according to EU standards, solve problems, and monitor implementation. Signing an SAA confers the status of "potential candidate for accession to the European Union" on the signatory. Thus far only Croatia and Macedonia have signed SAAs, while the remaining areas of the western Balkans—Albania, Bosnia and Herzegovina, Serbia and Montenegro, and Kosovo—are still in the preparatory phase for entering into negotiations. Non-signatory countries are nonetheless eligible for technical and financial assistance under the CARDS program, which provides financial support for the political, legal, and economic reforms and institution-building necessary to implement SAP obligations.

In addition to fostering bilateral relations between individual countries and the European Union, the SAP also emphasizes regional cooperation among the Balkan countries. As such, the SAP encourages the establishment of close informal and contractual relationships between the signatories of SAAs, akin to those between EU member states; aims to create a network of compatible bilateral free trade agreements; includes the gradual reintegration of the western Balkans into the infrastructure network of wider Europe; and urges the countries to cooperate on addressing security threats—to the Balkans and the European Union—that come from organized crime, illegal immigration, and other forms of trafficking. Approximately 10 percent of the CARDS budget will be directed toward this regional cooperation component, totalling €197 million ($193 million) in the period 2002–2004.

For more information, see the European Union's website: http://www.europa.eu.int/comm/external_relations/see/actions/index.htm.

II. NATO MEMBERSHIP ACTION PLAN AND PARTNERSHIP FOR PEACE

The NATO Membership Action Plan, initiated in April 1999, is an assistance program that provides advice and practical support to aspirant countries to the alliance. There are currently nine participants in MAP, including Slovenia, Albania, and Macedonia. While there is some overlap between MAP and NATO's Partnership for Peace, MAP does *not* supplant the PFP, and MAP participants are expected to maintain full participation in the PFP. The differences in the two programs can be understood this way. The PFP is a bilateral cooperation program between NATO and PFP countries, of which there are 26; its aims are to develop interoperability between the forces of aspirant countries and NATO forces, prepare aspirants' force structures and capabilities for possible future membership, and promote transparency in national defense planning and military budgeting. Conversely, MAP focuses less on interoperability and joint operations and more on establishing the guidelines and benchmarks that aspirant countries must keep within or fulfill in order to be considered for eventual membership, and providing assistance and expertise to help countries achieve these goals. It is important to note, however, that participation in MAP and the PFP does not guarantee future membership: accession negotiations proceed on a case-by-case basis and require a consensus within the alliance.

Four main elements are used to further MAP's agenda of advice, assistance, and practical support:

1) The annual submission by aspirant countries of individual national programs, outlining their preparations for possible future membership and covering political, economic, defense, resource, security, and legal aspects;

2) A focused feedback mechanism to appraise aspirant countries of their progress, including candid political and technical advice on their programs;

3) A clearinghouse to coordinate assistance by NATO and member states to aspirant countries in the area of defense;

4) A defense planning approach for aspirants, including elaboration and review of agreed-upon planning targets.

MAP places certain expectations on aspirant countries. In the political and economic arena, participants are expected to peacefully settle any international, ethnic, or external territorial disputes; establish civilian democratic control of their military; demonstrate a commitment to human rights and the rule of law; and promote a market economy. Defense and military issues, such as planning targets and interoperability issues, are primarily handled through the PFP (making MAP members' full participation in the PFP crucial). Aspirant countries are expected to commit sufficient resources to defense to enable them to meet the commitments (in terms of collective NATO operations) that future membership would entail. In the security field, expectations center around aspirant countries' ability to ensure the safety of sensitive information. Finally, legal aspects concern the need for aspirants to ensure compatibility between domestic legislation and the arrangements and agreements that govern cooperation within NATO.

For more information on the PFP, see http://www.nato.int/pfp/pfp.htm. For information on MAP, see http://www.nato.int/docu/handbook/2001/hb030103.htm.

Appendix A-2: Summary of International Objectives

	International Presence & Objectives	Rule of Law	Economic Restructuring	Refugees & Internally Displaced People	Civil Society & Media
Immediate 2002–2004	—Restructure the international objectives in the region toward the EU's SAP —Appoint an EU special envoy for the Balkans, with responsibility for the SAP; create a similar position in the U.S. State Department for policy coordination —Condition aid on the negotiation toward, and/or signature of, SAAs by all Balkan countries by 2004 —Initiate direct talks between Pristina and Belgrade on technical issues —Begin operations to combat politico-criminal syndicates	—Revise state and entity constitutions to remove discriminatory language —Continue aid conditionality on full cooperation with the ICTY —Establish a group donors conference, under the EU, to coordinate assistance for judicial system reform —Adopt anti-corruption and anti-organized crime legislation —Use donor funding and training programs to reform and upgrade the capacity and professionalism of the law enforcement and legal systems	—Establish systems of bank supervision —Enact into law financial regulatory standards on property rights, bankruptcy, and shareholders' rights —Continue or begin enterprise restructuring and privatization —Continue liberalization of trade and customs procedures consistent with EU standards —Rationalize tax regimes	—Rebuild physical infrastructure, particularly housing —Create and/or enforce procedural mechanisms for restitution of property —Adopt dual citizenship legislation —Establish a regional working group to address issues of pensions, property rights, compensation, and citizenship —Continue security assistance for refugees	—Enact measures granting legal status for NGOs —Begin the privatization or conversion (into public service organizations) of state-run media, particularly in Serbia —Work with Western partners on civil society development and training programs

Appendix A-2 (cont.)

	International Presence & Objectives	Rule of Law	Economic Restructuring	Refugees & Internally Displaced People	Civil Society & Media
Medium-term 2005–2007	—Prepare exit strategies for ad hoc international organizations in the Balkans and begin transition of operations to EU offices and local authorities —Prioritize cooperation with NATO's MAP and PFP programs —Determine final status for Kosovo —Continue indicting, arresting, and prosecuting those individuals involved in politico-criminal syndicates	—Conduct ICTY-led war crimes proceedings in the region and begin transferring jurisdiction to competent local tribunals —Enact and enforce anti-corruption and anti-organized crime legislation —Condition aid on the integration of ethnic minorities into police forces	—Establish business training programs using foreign private and public sector resources —Establish mortgage finance systems —Complete privatization and enterprise restructuring —In Kosovo, devolve registration, licensing, taxing, and enforcement functions to Kosovar institutions —In BiH, condition aid on the demand that, by 2005, there be only one finance ministry, customs authority, and banking regulatory agency for all of Bosnia	—Aid development among returned or integrated refugees through bilateral and multilateral initiatives focusing on job training and small and medium-sized enterprise development among refugees —Continue the procedure of recognition of property rights and property restitution —Condition aid on the acceptance and, where applicable, enactment into law of the recommendations of the regionwide working group	—Revise tax regimes to grant tax-exempt status for not-for-profit organizations. Grant discounts, refunds, and exemption from other taxes (such as a value-added tax) to NGOs —Complete privatization or conversion of state-owned media outlets —Continue funding and training for civil society development

Appendix A-2 (cont.)

	International Presence & Objectives	Rule of Law	Economic Restructuring	Refugees & Internally Displaced People	Civil Society & Media
Long-term 2008–2010	—Complete the transition from ad hoc institutions to indigenous institutions —Transfer the campaign against politico-criminal syndicates to local investigative units and police/security forces —Continue the streamlining and modernization process of Balkan militaries, in conjunction with NATO's MAP and PFP programs, including the restructuring of the BiH military	—Finish ICTY operations by 2008 (including the completion of the trials of Radovan Karadzic and Ratko Mladic) and continue in-country proceedings through 2010 —Continue to enhance local capacity (using bilateral and multilateral aid and direct operational assistance) to fight organized crime and prosecute cases fairly and effectively	—Reform pension systems along the lines of western European systems —Enact and implement laws on product liability —Continue to conform economic legislation and financial practices to EU standards	—Refugees have either returned to their homes or resettled in new areas to such an extent by 2010 that international organizations and NGOs can substantially reduce or close their offices in the region —Continue security protection for minority returnees as long as necessary	—Growing independence of indigenous NGOs, with continued, but lessened, assistance of international NGOs and democracy promotion organizations

APPENDIX A-3: UN MISSION IN KOSOVO "STANDARDS BEFORE STATUS" (MAY 2002)

From "Standards before Status," a publication of the UN Mission in Kosovo:

"One of my main responsibilities in implementing Resolution 1244 is to design a process to determine Kosovo's future status. We will not be able to get to this stage until Kosovo's society and institutions show that they are ready. Therefore, we must spell out what is required in order to get there. This is why I have devised a series of benchmarks that will identify what needs to be done before we can launch the discussions on status. Kosovo can only advance towards a fair and just society when these minimum pre-conditions are met. First standards then status. These standards also mirror those that are required to be considered for integration into Europe. On the one hand they represent the beginnings of an exit strategy for the international community, but they are also in reality an entry strategy into Europe."

—*Michael Steiner*
Special Representative of the Secretary-General

Appendix A-3: UN Mission in Kosovo "Standards before Status" (May 2002)

	Goals	Benchmarks	Action by Local Entities
Functioning Democratic Institutions	—Democratic governance —Revenue collection and efficient delivery of public services —Minority political participation and access to public services and public employment consolidated —Full implementation of undertakings in government coalition agreement (February 28) —PISG in authority throughout Kosovo	—Effective, representative, and functioning institutions of government authority in all Kosovo —Promotion of civil society structures, human rights, and full participation by women —Lead role by PISG in policy setting —Transparency in the allocation of resources —Meaningful participation by minority civil servants in government —Responsible and professional media	—Accountability through focus on delivery of public services —Proportionate minority representation in government —PISG to work in both official languages —Align and develop legislation to EU and international standards —Participation by women in government
Rule of Law (Police/ Judiciary)	—Organized crime networks disrupted, financial crime checked, and end of extremist violence —Public respect for police and judiciary —Impartiality of judges and Kosovo Police Service (KPS), prosecution of all suspected criminals, and fair trial guaranteed to everyone —Sufficient minority representation	—Extremism not tolerated by mainstream —International judges and police enabled to take supportive function —Increased reliability of, and prosecution of crime by, Kosovo judiciary —Customs service and KPS participate in anti–organized crime strategy —KPS recognized as reliable partner internationally	—Sustained effort by PISG to promote values of rule of law —Holders of public office to abstain from extremist public statements —PISG budget support to promote higher education and entrance examinations in legal field

Appendix A-3 (cont.)

	Goals	Benchmarks	Action by Local Entities
Freedom of Movement	—All communities can circulate freely throughout Kosovo, including city centers, and use their language	—Unrestricted movement by minorities without reliance on military or police	—Policy and sustained action by PISG to promote freedom of movement publicly —Unprompted condemnation by holders of public office of obstruction and violence
Returns and Reintegration	—All Kosovo inhabitants have a right to remain, right to property, and right to return respected throughout Kosovo	—Conditions for safe and sustainable returns and reintegration created —All IDPs and refugees have necessary information for decisions on returns —Returns to urban areas have started —Adequate allocation of budget resources by PISG for returns and reintegration	—Active advocacy by political and community leaders for returns and reintegration, hosting of go-and-see visits —Key Kosovo-Albanian leaders to have participated in go-and-inform visits where IDPs live —Budget allocation by PISG for returns and reintegration
Economy	—Sound institutional and legal basis for a market economy —Balanced budget —Privatization of socially owned assets	—Minimum legal and regulatory framework to secure investment —Improved tax and revenue collection —Progress on privatization	—Support for establishment of solid economic framework —Active public support for privatization by holders of public office
Property Rights	—All property, including residential property, land, enterprises, and other socially owned assets, will have a clear and rightful owner	—Significant progress in repossession of properties	—Compliance with and support of the Housing and Property Directorate (HPD) adjudications —PISG and municipal support for evictions —Kosovo budget contribution to HPD

Appendix A-3 (cont.)

	Goals	Benchmarks	Action by Local Entities
Dialogue with Belgrade	—Normal relations with Belgrade, and eventually with other neighboring areas	—Practical issues addressed through direct contacts —Problems solved through dialogue and correspondence —Business relations restarted	—PISG participation in High-Ranking Working Group —Reciprocity in PISG visiting Belgrade and welcoming visitors to Pristina
Kosovo Protection Corps (KPC)	—Contingent reduced to numbers commensurate with its mandate —Minority participation	—Appropriately reduced contingent —Unqualified compliance with KPC mandate —Relations established with all communities and proportionate minority representation	—Active endorsement by public officeholders of reduced KPC numbers and participation of minorities

General Prerequisites: Full compliance with and implementation of Resolution 1244 and the Constitutional Framework. Multiethnicity, tolerance, security, and fairness under normal conditions, without special measures.

APPENDIX B: TRANSITIONAL JUSTICE, PUBLIC SECURITY, AND THE RULE OF LAW

I. INTRODUCTION

Putting an end to armed conflict in the Balkans was difficult; building stable countries that will grow economically and assume a place in a united Europe is equally difficult. It cannot be accomplished without the rule of law.

"Rule of law" is a shorthand term for a legal system in which justice is administered openly and fairly according to prescribed statutes and regulations; individuals and organizations are held accountable; judges are impartial; minority rights are protected; access to the courts is available to all; and legitimate court rulings are enforced. It encompasses both criminal and civil law, the latter being crucial for economic development.[23]

Establishing the rule of law in the territory of the former Yugoslavia requires that the local governments hold war criminals accountable; reform ethnically biased police forces and judiciaries; establish fair, transparent, efficient, and professional criminal and civil justice systems; and combat organized crime and corruption. Absent vigorous and respectable legal systems, the Balkan region faces the prospect of unremitting ethnic tension, further economic failure, and the continued growth of organized crime. Full integration into Europe will remain a chimera.

But so far the local and international actors in the region have not accorded the rule of law the high status it deserves. Remedying this problem will require the determination of the Balkan governments

---

[23] Among other things, economic development in the Balkan states requires legislation to reform banking, remove barriers to trade, and establish transparent systems of business regulation. Current commercial codes and financial regulations are also outdated or nonexistent and need to be drafted and/or modernized and enforced. The pervasive corruption in the legal and business communities also needs tackling. For more information on the relationship between economic development and the rule of law, see Appendix C.

and the dedication, technical assistance, and resources of key international actors. Particularly important are the European Union (through its Stabilization and Association Process), the International Criminal Tribunal for the former Yugoslavia (ICTY), the United States, the UN Mission in Kosovo (UNMIK), the Office of the High Representative (OHR) in Bosnia, the Organization for Security and Cooperation in Europe (OSCE), the World Bank, and NGOs specializing in legal reform, such as the American Bar Association's Central and East European Law Initiative (CEELI).

The Task Force believes that establishing the rule of law is the number one priority for the prevention of future violence and the evolution of the Balkan states into stable, modern countries. For all Balkan governments and international agencies, the standards and objectives laid out in the EU's Stabilization and Association Process (SAP) provide the best overall guide for adapting policies and strategies to strengthen the rule of law. As such, this framework is the proper model for allocation of resources and implementation of reforms; the UNMIK law enforcement "pillar" in Kosovo is a useful example of how this model can be put to use.

II. TRANSITIONAL JUSTICE

The meting out of transitional justice—an imprecise but crucial process of legal proceedings and collective soul-searching by which a society comes to terms with its past—is an indispensable step on the path to Europe for each Balkan state. Transitional justice is intended to hold war criminals accountable, prevent the reemergence of authoritarian power structures, and encourage reconciliation. This process, however painful, cannot be avoided, and it cannot be completed quickly or arbitrarily.

A necessary first step is the removal, by national and regional legislatures, of all discriminatory provisions from constitutions and statutes. This task can be accomplished by the end of 2004, especially if international donors compel it through the use of conditionality. UNMIK and the OHR can also use their discretion to ensure that the necessary amendments are adopted.

Nine years after the UN Security Council established the ICTY in The Hague, many of the people who were responsible for ethnic cleansing, destruction of property, and murder are still at large, or even in positions of authority. It is imperative that decisive action be taken on these cases—including those of Radovan Karadzic and Ratko Mladic—by the responsible authorities in all jurisdictions within the next six to twelve months. This is crucial for the sake of justice in the Balkan states, and to encourage the return of minorities displaced during the war.[24] Conditioning aid upon full and timely cooperation with the ICTY is the proper stick for donors—including governments and international organizations such as the European Union—to use in order to ensure compliance, including the prompt arrest of suspects, delivery of witnesses, and access to documents. The political influence of the European Union, the United States, and international institutions can also be effectively used with individual governments to extract commitments to the tribunal. Unfortunately, until now only the United States has conditioned assistance on cooperation with the tribunal.

The Task Force strongly believes that The Hague tribunal is a critical participant in the region's efforts to establish transitional justice. It alone has the capacity to conduct impartial, professional investigations and prosecutions across ethnic, national, religious, and racial lines. Domestic court systems are not yet credible enough to properly handle these offenses.

However, certain changes in the way the ICTY conducts its business are warranted. The ICTY can function more openly, lifting the veil of secrecy—both surrounding the events of the 1990s and the work of the tribunal—as much as possible. This entails diminishing the use of secret indictments, except where secrecy is nec-

---

[24] There is evidence to suggest a relationship between the apprehension of indicted war criminals and refugee return. For example, in Prijedor, Bosnia and Herzegovina, the houses of displaced Muslims were targets of organized arson in 1996. The next year, several indicted war criminals were arrested in the area, and minority returns began after the arrests. A few years later, Prijedor was the site of the first rebuilt mosque in Republika Srpska. The arrest of war criminals reduced the fear of further persecution, and it sent a signal that people responsible for atrocities were being held accountable.

essary to ensure the capture of suspects, and establishing procedures to make public all government records pertaining to the conflicts of the 1990s, except where their release would infringe on either the rights of the parties in the tribunal or agreements made with those providing information. Both of these reforms can be in effect by the end of 2004. Cooperation on the latter reform can be included in the conditionality regimes enforced by donor states and organizations.

Compelling compliance with the tribunal is one matter; changing peoples' attitudes toward the ICTY is more difficult. Negative public opinion of the tribunal—not helped by the performance of Slobodan Milosevic at his trial—has made governments wary of cooperating. In certain countries—notably Serbia and Bosnia— a defensive alliance has been formed between nationalist politicians, organized criminal elements, and war criminals in order to retain some power in governance or, at least, remain out of reach. The ICTY can take steps to combat the negative impression of its mission. One way is setting up forums such as town hall–style meetings with NGOs and local governments to engage the local citizens and explain the ICTY process.

The Task Force also believes that the ICTY can strengthen the process of transitional justice in the Balkans by conducting proceedings (including, if possible, entire trials) in the region so that people can see impartial justice being done, and by transferring proceedings and jurisdiction to competent local tribunals. We therefore strongly recommend that these actions be taken as soon as possible, realistically between 2005 and 2007.

For these recommendations to be enacted, it is imperative that indigenous capacity be strengthened. Current court systems throughout the region have proved incapable of meting out fair and equal justice in cases involving local citizens who were not prominent enough to be tried by the ICTY.[25] Empanelling international

---

[25] Illustrative examples in this regard include Kosovo, where the OSCE and other international monitors have documented cases of Serbs convicted on shaky evidence, Albanians set free despite substantial evidence against them, and Croatia, where Serbs accused of war crimes have been subject to excessive pre-trial detention and often do not receive fair trials.

judges to resolve these issues, as is being done in Kosovo, is an acceptable but short-term resolution to this problem. The ICTY can help improve local capacity by sponsoring, in cooperation with donors such as the European Union, the training of indigenous judicial and law enforcement personnel.

Given the scope of the tasks that still confront the ICTY, the allocation by the UN Security Council of additional resources to the tribunal is strongly recommended.

Transitional justice cannot simply be confined to a courtroom in the Netherlands. The process will unfold most effectively if governments establish formal mechanisms to confront their societies with facts that have been uncovered. The objective is to develop systems of transitional justice that enable society to come to terms with the past and that demonstrate justice has been done.[26] These systems may include prosecutions, but they may also include alternatives such as truth commissions, which have been employed successfully elsewhere.[27] Nongovernmental groups, including representatives of aggrieved minorities, can work with governments to develop a process that gains public acceptance. Organizations such as the International Center for Transitional Justice (ICTJ), the U.S. Institute of Peace (USIP), and the International Human Rights Law Group (IHRLG) can provide technical assistance.

III. PUBLIC SECURITY AND IMPARTIAL JUSTICE

A second critical milestone on the road to joining Europe is the establishment of domestic justice and law enforcement systems that treat all citizens equally.

---

[26] It is fundamental that all proceedings and inquiries related to the ethnic conflicts of the past decade target individuals, not groups, to make clear that ethnic or religious communities as a whole are not guilty. It is also important that systems of transitional justice be insulated against vindictiveness and vigilante justice. Human rights groups, citizen watchdogs, and international observers can be enlisted to monitor proceedings, participate in decisions, and help ensure that the deliberations are transparent.

[27] In Serbia, a Truth Commission has been established but does not enjoy wide support from the human rights community; in Bosnia there has been an ongoing attempt to establish a similar commission, but it still lacks political support.

The judicial and law enforcement systems in the region share certain undesirable characteristics. Minority rights are problematic, with minority groups subject to unfair treatment by prosecutors and judges. And the police are often part of the problem, rather than the solution: police forces are poorly trained and equipped, have little investigative capacity, are unintegrated, and are often tainted with a record of ethnic bias. Judges are underpaid and undertrained, criminal procedure codes are inefficient, and court rulings are often politicized and frequently ignored even when valid. Court systems are overburdened and lacking in resources, characterized by large case backlogs, and hampered by weak administrative support. Corruption is endemic and encouraged by the low salaries that prevail among law enforcement and judicial personnel.

Fixing these problems will require a concerted effort by local governments and significant resources from international actors. The European Union is the proper institution to lead this endeavor, and has in fact committed itself to provide resources and technical assistance toward these ends through various institution-building and Justice and Home Affairs programs funded by the CARDS scheme.[28] The U.S. Agency for International Development is another crucial participant and already has experience in developing the rule of law as part of its democracy and governance programs. In terms of police reform, the OSCE and UN missions in Bosnia and Kosovo are the foremost agencies; in the future, the EU police mission is also expected to figure prominently. In Bosnia and Kosovo, the OHR and UNMIK, respectively, will also be heavily involved.

Given the scope of the necessary reforms, it is vital that sufficient funding be assured. The Task Force therefore recommends that a consultative group donors conference be organized, under the EU's leadership and by the end of 2003, in order to coordi-

---

[28] The Community Assistance for Reconstruction, Development, and Stabilization (CARDS) program is the financial assistance program that underpins the EU's Stabilization and Association Process. See Appendix A-1.

nate assistance and delegate responsibilities among governments and institutions.

A number of priority actions are required for the successful reform of the law enforcement and judicial systems in the region. The entire justice system, civil and criminal, requires independence from political and criminal interference. Necessary steps to promote this end include the provision of adequate pay packages for judges, prosecutors, and public defenders; the adoption of clear and transparent selection criteria for all personnel; adherence to the recommendations of the European Association of Judges "Monitoring Committee"; and the removal from office of persons responsible for past abuses. The appropriate international bodies—the EU and the OSCE in Macedonia, Serbia and Montenegro, and, where still required, in Croatia; the OHR through the Independent Judicial Commission (IJC) and the Criminal Justice Advisory Unit in Bosnia; and the Kosovo Judicial and Prosecutorial Council and Judicial Inspection Unit in Kosovo—can oversee and assist with these actions. If necessary, they can also coordinate with other donors, including the international financial institutions, to assist the state governments with funding for these ends.

The development of codes of conduct and standards of ethical behavior in the judicial systems is also necessary.[29] The OSCE, Council of Europe, bar associations, and NGOs can advise local authorities on the necessary steps. In particular, the establishment of judiciary ombudsmen to liaise between the justice ministries and the courts will help to set standards, coordinate training, and assure accountability through peer monitoring.

Training at all levels is urgently required. It can be accomplished through the enactment of rigorous bilateral or multilateral training programs for judges, attorneys, and police, with penalties mandated by the local governments for those who do not participate in a timely manner; and through the establishment of programs to provide technical advice and cooperation on legal system and code reforms. The development of a strategic training plan and curriculum, with an emphasis on practical, skill-based train-

---

[29] UNMIK has already promulgated codes of conduct in Kosovo.

ing, is vital. Joint programs on investigative skills and related legal provisions are also critical for police, prosecutors, and investigative judges. Training programs must necessarily accord with European standards and include instruction in the standards of justice and human rights embedded in the European Convention on Human Rights. The training programs convened under UNMIK's Pillar I in Kosovo, conducted by UNMIK and the OSCE, can serve as useful models.

As noted above, the European Union is expected to be the key participant in, and coordinator of, these actions, in cooperation with local authorities. The ICTY can also be usefully tapped to train advocates and judges, as can NGOs such as CEELI, which already conducts training programs throughout the Balkan region. For police training, the OSCE, UNMIK, and the UN Mission in Bosnia and Herzegovina (UNMIBH) are the prominent actors.

Full-scale reform of police forces is also necessary. This requires the regional governments to reduce bloated forces by accelerating early retirement and cashiering inefficient or corrupt officials (using information from international and local human rights organizations). It also mandates the ethnic integration of police forces. The hiring of more ethnic minorities by police forces is vital to enhance community security and encourage minority returns, and the UN, the EU, and the OSCE need to publicize and monitor the process to ensure that it is properly conducted. After a grace period, government donors and the EU can condition aid on the ongoing integration of ethnic minorities into policing. International technical and financial support will also be required to devise institutional mechanisms of accountability for police forces, and to ensure that forces are adequately equipped.

Beyond the common circumstances listed above, individual countries face their own challenges to the establishment of viable, impartial judicial and law enforcement systems.

In Serbia, where some progress in judicial reform has been made under the new government, military courts still retain a legal mandate and often intervene in what are properly civilian matters, to the extent of indicting and trying civilians for defaming the military or revealing supposed state secrets.[30] Furthermore, according to its doctrine, the Yugoslav Army (VJ) retains significant responsibility for maintaining internal stability and security; as such, its intelligence services are actively involved in Serb internal politics. The VJ has used this discretion to undermine the Serb government by thwarting cooperation with the ICTY and, in the winter of 2002, arresting a deputy minister and a U.S. diplomat—an act that was an outright challenge to constitutional order. Serious structural reform of the VJ—and the Serbian Ministry of the Interior (MUP), which also handles internal security—is required. Both bodies are corrupt and opposed to internal and societal reform, and the VJ resists budget transparency. However, given that the VJ is consistently rated the most respected institution among the Serb people, challenging it is tricky. Encouragingly, elements of the Serbian government have expressed willingness to join NATO's Partnership for Peace (PFP), a stance that the Task Force strongly recommends. Participation in the PFP would give the government a crucial tool with which to establish civilian democratic control over the military and halt the VJ's improper intervention in civilian judicial affairs.

Serbia and Montenegro are also dogged by constitutional issues. The federal republic has for some time been mostly a paper entity, and the leaders of Serbia and Montenegro have agreed to restructure their relationship in a way that largely frees them to operate independently of each other. But until the two parliaments—and the federal parliament—ratify and implement the March 2002 status agreement, the federal republic's Milosevic-era constitution remains in effect, and the federal government retains some functions that have limited the freedom of its two constituent republics to take effective action on transitional justice and legal reform. It remains to be seen whether the new constitution of Ser-

---

[30] Notable among the reforms were the enactment of salary increases for judges in the autumn of 2001, and the concomitant decision by the Serbian Ministry of Justice to remove judges and prosecutors for violations of law, abuse of their positions, or failure to meet professional standards.

bia and Montenegro, adopted in August 2002 following the status agreement of March 2002, will effectively resolve these issues.

The effort to build the rule of law in Kosovo—overseen by UNMIK's Pillar I for police and justice issues, which consolidates into a single structure the international supervision of, and participation in, law enforcement and judicial affairs in Kosovo—is complicated by the tenuous security situation in the area. Beyond the basic security provided by the NATO Kosovo Force (KFOR) troops, Kosovo also hosts an international civilian police force of more than 4,000 officers and a locally recruited Kosovo Police Service (KPS), both under the administration of the UN. By January 2002, there were 4,392 KPS officers, of whom 375, or 8.5 percent, were Kosovo Serbs. These forces are doing a satisfactory job but, like forces elsewhere in the region, are undertrained and lack sufficient resources. The KPS's legitimacy is also undermined by suspicion that some members are primarily loyal to political parties and to former Kosovo Liberation Army (KLA) commanders. Moreover, while KFOR tends to measure security in terms of number of incidents, Kosovo Serbs measure it by their actual freedom of movement and freedom to participate in the structures of daily life. Seen in this light, the security situation in Kosovo is much graver.

The role of the Kosovo Protection Corps (KPC), a civilian defense organization reconstructed from the KLA, is particularly problematic. The KPC's mission is nominally nonmilitary but has never been clearly defined, a failure that requires remedy. Moreover, some of its members are reputedly involved in organized crime and have provided support to ethnic Albanian insurgent movements elsewhere in the region. This lack of accountability is unacceptable. An important corrective step that UNMIK can take is to sack KPC members proven to have engaged in illegal or insurgent activity. Continued funding of the KPC by the United States and UNMIK needs to be contingent upon accountability and responsible conduct.

In Bosnia, meanwhile, the complex political architecture combined with limited and inconsistent action by the international community has inhibited the successful establishment of the rule of law.[31] For example, each of the country's two entities—the Federation of Bosnia and Herzegovina and Republika Srpska—maintains its own police force, with minimal interentity cooperation; both forces have remained stubbornly resistant to the efforts, during the past three years, of the UN special representative of the secretary-general with respect to police reform. In particular, the process of de-authorization of unfit, biased, or corrupt police (with full international oversight) remains necessary. It is crucial that the UN Mission in Bosnia's mandate with respect to policing be vigorously enforced through the end of 2002 and be handed off without a slip to the European Union Police Mission (EUPM), fulfilling the obligations for minority recruitment, professionalization, and basic cooperation that are crucial to protecting all citizens.

Bosnia has a number of experienced, talented advocates and judges but has been slow to develop an independent, impartial, and professional court system. There has been little progress in building nationwide judicial and bar associations, with the result that legal practice differs greatly within the country. Entity courts, for example, remain the courts of first instance for most routine civil and criminal proceedings. These courts are often partial, ill-equipped, and subject to influence by local political elites, hampering both routine proceedings and the prosecution of sophisticated organized crime. The Task Force therefore believes that the OHR needs to initiate the creation of a central court system with nationwide jurisdiction.

The international community has devoted substantial resources to training Bosnia's judiciary and preparing its institutions. On the

---

[31] There have been positive developments. For example, the completion in 2001 of the Independent Judicial Commission's overall strategy for the justice sector was a step toward a more coherent national and international structure. The central government also has a nascent investigative and enforcement service and increasing ability to enforce the nation's immigration and customs laws. Many crucial institutions and laws are formally in place; constructive Bosnian figures are gaining political authority; and—perhaps most important—the ability of corrupt elites to obstruct international implementation efforts is diminishing.

whole, the essential activities carried out by judicial personnel are professional and well done. They are no substitute, however, for a robust investigative capacity or the political will to confront powerful obstructionists. More important, the piecemeal screening of judges by the peer review commission, which has recently been scrapped by the Peace Implementation Council (which oversees the OHR's work), means that a full-scale reappointment process for all judges is required.

The OHR will continue to be the lead international player in the development of the rule of law in Bosnia. The Task Force recommends that the OHR continue pressing for the passage of uniform criminal and civil legislation in both entities; the enactment of effective and fair legal procedures, criminal investigations, civil litigation, and judicial processes; and the establishment of a single judicial space and implementation of the Constitutional Court's decision on the equality of the "constituent peoples."[32] These tasks can be completed by the end of 2004.

IV. ORGANIZED CRIME

Organized crime continues to be a social and economic cancer in the body politic. Economic activity is often characterized by smuggling, extortion, and tax evasion that undermine the ability of the region's new governments to stabilize their economies, collect revenue, and attract investment. The economic and political power wielded by criminal syndicates often makes them attractive to young people who are unable to find work in the legitimate marketplace, thus perpetuating the problem.

---

[32] A major achievement was the completion in April 2002 of interentity, interparty, and international negotiation on implementing the court decision in the "constituent peoples" case. The final decisions, including the high representative's imposition of relatively few, but important, changes to assure representation of ethnic minorities in the court system, are crucial steps forward. The implementation of the constituent peoples decision may turn out to be a major step toward providing for the equality of constituent peoples in both entities, and to fair representation in the federation government structures.

In Serbia, Milosevic's military-political-mafia complex contributed to the criminalization of society, destroyed the middle class, and plundered the country of most of its assets. Even now, the police are often involved in criminal activities, and judges and justice are too often for sale.[33] In Bosnia, the reforms in justice and in the police have been limited and piecemeal. Many Task Force members believe that there is a greater danger of the state being taken over by organized crime than of a return to ethnically based internal war.

These conditions make it difficult to confront the criminal organizations that thrived in the Balkans during the 1990s. Breaking the grip of these organizations will require the international community to be aggressive, committed, and directly involved in police actions, investigations, and prosecutions. As the European Union works to bring the Balkan countries up to standards that would make them candidates for membership, any country that fails to decisively address the problems of organized crime and the lack of rule of law will remain a threat to the stability of the entire region. Some of the problems that led to the violence of the past decade have been contained rather than solved; to strengthen institutions of justice and promote the rule of law, it is essential that these matters are settled in a peaceful manner.

Recognizing that entrenched corruption and organized crime in the Balkans represent a threat to all of Europe—and that, with Slovenia on a fast track to EU membership, Croatia will soon become a front-line state on the EU's border—the European Union has stated its commitment to help the countries of southeastern Europe combat corruption. The EU program includes assistance in drafting anti-corruption and money laundering legislation, training judges and police forces, bolstering customs services, and reforming government procurement procedures. Close monitoring of government procurement procedures by the World

---

[33] The reformist government in Serbia has made some strides in addressing corruption and organized crime, but its progress remains uneven. The clearest example of this is the law on extra profit, which requires many Milosevic cronies who took in illegal gains during the 1990s to pay retroactive taxes on those gains. While some ill-gotten funds have been recovered from Milosevic-era officials, civic groups complain that the government has failed to account for the funds it has recouped.

Bank and other donors is also necessary, and these donors can condition balance of payments and other budget support on transparency, accountability, and enforcement of anti-corruption measures. Donors can also provide support for international monitors helping local ombudsmen and inspector-general offices to pursue corruption, and for civil society efforts to spotlight corruption.

The U.S. Department of Justice, and NGOs such as Transparency International and CEELI, can be enlisted to help draft anti-corruption legislation. Border security is an issue of particular importance. Ensuring border security and building adequate capacity for monitoring customs regulations will require considerable cooperation among local governments, and between the region and the EU.[34] Adoption of extradition and legal assistance treaties between Western and Balkan countries is also necessary.

However, taking on entrenched criminal syndicates and prosecuting participants will require a more aggressive approach by the international community. The first task is to understand the nature and scope of the problem and to identify participants. Credible governing authorities, whether duly elected or internationally appointed, can assign assessment teams of experienced prosecutors, law enforcement units, and, perhaps, military personnel to evaluate the law enforcement and statutory system in each country. Of particular relevance are the existing investigative capabilities; prosecutorial competence; the viability of witness protection systems; search warrant and asset seizure procedures; money laundering laws; financial disclosure requirements; and treaties on extradition and mutual legal assistance. Deploying these teams as a priority matter will indicate strong determination to identify and uproot entrenched criminal elements.

If these assessment teams determine that local prosecutors and judges lack the capacity to take on criminal syndicates, or fear to do so because of threats and intimidation, there are other

---

[34] Such cooperation is, in fact, already underway. In November 2001, the EU brokered an agreement for regional cooperation—which included Slovenia and Croatia—in combating organized crime, drug smuggling, and human trafficking. The agreement identifies EU norms and commits the signatories to abide by standard practices of the EU.

options. One is to create a cadre of international judges, as has been done in Kosovo. Alternatively, suspects may be transferred to another country, which might claim jurisdiction if the alleged criminal activity crossed its borders.

Assuming that local officials are willing to undertake investigations and prosecutions, they can be insulated from political interfererence by making clear to the public how the investigative and prosecutorial teams are funded, whom they are answerable to, who can hire and fire them, and what their mission is.

International intervention to counter obstructionism and organized crime is a difficult, but far from impossible, task. Indeed, experience in Bosnia has shown that direct, forceful action by the international community brings progress. In 2000 and early 2001, a brief campaign in Bosnia led by the international community did more damage to the politico-criminal syndicates there than any single action since the conclusion of the Dayton Agreement. For example, forced closure of banks linked to the hard-line Croation Democratic Party (HDZ) and organized crime elements in Herzegovina—with the OHR giving the order to shut down the syndicates and SFOR charged with providing crowd control and security to enforce the decision—was encouraging, even if implementation was flawed. The lack of adequate planning or force presence by SFOR led, at least initially, to the perception that the targeted syndicates could defy the international community. But in the end they were forced to yield. Other, more positive, examples include a raid on the Republika Srpska interior forces in August 1997, seizure of television stations controlled by the hard-line Serb Democratic Party (SDS) in September 1997, and the installation of a non-SDS government in Republika Srpska in 1999. A 1999 raid on an HDZ-controlled illegal market was followed by the first fissures in the Croat political hierarchy, an investigation of illegal campaign finances, and the removal from government and corporate structures of key HDZ officials.

The pattern is unmistakable: Robust measures, aimed at the levers of power controlled by nationalist groups, produce results. Twenty thousand NATO troops control the strategic environment and make law-enforcement action possible; fifty well-trained police officers protecting reliable auditors at a financial institution can make real progress toward reform.

In Bosnia, the OHR will continue to require the capability to bring sufficient force to bear on the kingpins of organized crime, either through its own police capacity or through multiethnic vetted strike forces of local police equipped with modern technology, trained and mentored by international police, and supported by military police units from SFOR. Elsewhere, the ability of local authorities to fight organized crime will be significantly improved by the active participation of the OSCE and the European Union Police Mission, in cooperation with Interpol; these agencies can provide direct operational assessment and assistance in the investigation and prosecution of criminal activity. The Task Force supports the decision of High Representative Paddy Ashdown to establish special chambers within the Court of Bosnia and the BiH Prosecution Office to deal specifically with organized crime, economic crime, and corruption. International judges may be appointed as needed.

APPENDIX C: ECONOMIC RESTRUCTURING AND DEVELOPMENT

I. INTRODUCTION

At this pivotal moment in their histories, the nations of the Balkans have only two choices for their economic future. They can embrace the prospect of formal economic association with the European Union, move steadily toward EU standards of governance and economic performance, and lay the groundwork for full participation in a united Europe and a globalized world economy. Or they can adhere to outdated economic models and continue to allow past practices of governance and ethnic conflict to set their agendas, relegating themselves to the poor margins of Europe.[35]

---

[35] Of the jurisdictions considered in this report, only Croatia is apparently sufficiently committed to, and far enough along on, a positive economic course to inspire confidence about its readiness to join the EU. Croatia's financial condition is better than that of the other Balkan nations treated in this report. Until very recently, this had less to do with Croatia's pursuit of good economic policies than with the fact that Croatia is naturally blessed with abundant sun and a long, clean coastline on the Adriatic—one of the few remaining in southern Europe—which attracts tourism that contributes at least $4 billion annually to the balance of payments. This figure could grow considerably higher if Croatia develops a plan for tourism that upgrades existing tourist facilities, improves management, and better advertises the country's considerable attractions. Under Franjo Tudjman's leadership throughout most of the 1990s, little economic reform occurred and interenterprise debts soared as companies were required to respond to the government's political priorities. The well-developed foreign trading relationships of many Croatian enterprises suffered or were badly compromised during this period. Despite substantial foreign investor interest in Croatia's enterprises and tourist assets, the Croatian government was reluctant to sell to foreigners, though some small deals were concluded with businessmen of Croatian ancestry. Unfortunately, some of the same concerns about foreign ownership of good Croatian companies remain in the thinking of the present government. However, one bright spot has been the sale of most Croatian banks to reputable foreign financial groups (principally Austrian, German, and Italian) that have cleaned up their balance sheets. These banks now are poised to support private sector growth, which could take off with concerted implementation of a privatization plan. Croatia has signed a Stabilization and Association Agreement, and its pro-Europe rhetoric is strong. Croatia can use the SAA process to progress to more tangible expressions of its commitment to join Europe.

The Council on Foreign Relations issued a Task Force report in 2000 entitled *Promoting Sustainable Economies in the Balkans.* This appendix builds on that report, particularly regarding property rights, privatization and enterprise reform, the use of conditionality, legal aspects of economic reform, and threats to economic progress posed by corruption and organized crime.

However, major changes have occurred since that report was issued. Most important, Slobodan Milosevic is in The Hague instead of Belgrade. The Serbian government, no longer isolated, is reforming and cooperating with the European Union and international financial institutions including the World Bank, the International Monetary Fund (IMF), the European Bank for Reconstruction and Development (EBRD), and the European Investment Bank (EIB). Furthermore, several of the policies advocated at the time of the 2000 report—including reform of the banking and financial systems—are now being implemented. Finally, the 2000 report reflected unease about the strength of Europe's commitment to the region and emphasized the need for the EU to formulate a concrete, step-by-step integration program. Now the EU has made a firm commitment to the Balkans, and emphasis has shifted to implementation.

The European Union is the lead organization coordinating most Western financial assistance to the Balkan reform effort. The EU gets considerable help from the World Bank through the joint World Bank/European Commission Office on Southeast Europe, but with so many different agencies of various governments involved in the effort, the managerial task of implementing such a huge economic project remains daunting. There is a genuine question whether local actors can contend with such multifarious demands and agendas. The Task Force therefore advises the European Union to increase its cooperation and coordination with all Western donors, so that its requirements are clear, coherent, achievable, and logically compelling to the local governments. This effort cannot succeed without host governments being invested in the reform process and willing to take responsibility for its ultimate success. The Task Force also recommends that the European Union spearhead the effort, in cooperation with the international financial institutions and bilateral donors, to create coherent conditions for assistance with economic reform. This conditionality regime will properly focus on measures to build the institutional infrastructure of a market economy and to narrow the possibilities for corruption.

The goal of the EU's effort to support economic reform is to help the Balkan states establish conditions for private investment and the successful operation of a market economy, so that jobs are created, trading relationships are revived and expanded, and living and educational standards are improved. Success in this endeavor is crucial; otherwise it will be difficult, if not impossible, to make substantial progress on the other pillars of political and civil society that are the foundation of a viable democracy.

Acceleration and completion of bank reform and enterprise restructuring and privatization are required. The development of the private sector is to be encouraged, through business training programs and access to credit from lending vehicles specially established to support worthy projects of small and medium-sized enterprises. It is also necessary that trade and customs procedures be liberalized in Balkan countries, consistent with EU standards, and free trade agreements be signed with other Balkan states that are compatible with World Trade Organization (WTO) agreements. Reform of financial sector legislation to make it clear and enforceable, and improvements in physical and financial infrastructures, are also important and costly tasks that are crucial to a trade and investment promotion strategy.[36]

So far, Balkan leaders have been disappointed with European leadership because promised assistance too often has been delayed by sluggish bureaucracy, slow disbursement rates, and ineffectual implementation.[37] The European Union has an interest in cor-

---

[36] As part of the Stabilization and Association Process, the European Union's CARDS program can provide technical and financial assistance for customs and trade matters, infrastructure repair, and business development programs. Physical security is another factor that affects both investment and trade. As noted in the Executive Summary and Appendixes A and B, the Task Force considers the continuation of NATO's missions and presence in the region to be essential.

[37] For example, at least $300 million promised in 2001 from the EIB, an EU agency, to rebuild Serbia's damaged infrastructure has not materialized, though Serbia was

recting these failings because they undermine the required negotiating leverage with local actors. Adherence to mutually agreed conditions for disbursements is particularly important for maintaining the confidence of both sides in the value of their engagement. The Task Force also encourages the EU to work with its member states to create a more cohesive strategy for their own bilateral aid programs, which seem to reflect their respective national objectives rather than local priorities such as agriculture.[38] For instance, currently some member states require that the aid they give be spent on projects with their own nationals in local joint venture investments.

Despite its much smaller financial contributions, the United States is regarded as the linchpin of reform in the Balkans, and every country wants the United States to maintain a prominent presence in the economic reform effort. It is important for the United States to continue providing bilateral economic assistance, but the most important economic role for the United States is to remain engaged with its European partners on managing the transition, coaxing and exhorting their leadership to fulfill the vision of a united Europe that includes the Balkans. Given the relatively small amount of U.S. bilateral aid (compared to that from the EU), it is important that the bilateral aid the U.S. does give be targeted to its priorities, such as establishing the rule of law, strengthening governing institutions, and supporting civil society.

II. CREATING THE CONDITIONS FOR INVESTMENT AND PROMOTING TRADE IN THE BALKANS

Building an economy capable of providing employment, producing competitive goods and services, attracting investment, and improving living standards requires a system of financial intermediation and supervision that dispenses credit competently and operates reli-

---

obliged to repay $230 million in past-due payments to regain access to that organization.

[38] The agricultural sector continues to be a major employer throughout the Balkans and is an area in which most Balkan countries could have competitive promise, given some managerial and technical assistance and generous access to European markets.

ably, according to a set of transparent rules under independent financial supervision codified by laws that are enforced equitably.

This is particularly urgent in the Balkans, where all the nations that emerged from the dissolution of Yugoslavia shared the legacy of an insolvent and poorly managed banking system, distrusted by a public that lost personal savings in these institutions over the last twenty years. Many of the new banks created in the 1990s perpetuated the same abusive practices. Furthermore, there are no domestic capital markets that can alternatively mobilize capital.

In an economically stable country, credit—the lifeblood of a market economy—is funded foremost by domestic savings placed on deposit with financial institutions. However, in the Balkans, until recently, most savings remained "under the mattress," unavailable for mobilization by banks to finance legitimate projects. Given the high unemployment and poverty rates throughout the region, the need to mobilize domestic savings cannot be overstated.

The conversion of most European currencies to the euro at the beginning of 2002 potentially represented an enormous opportunity to collect domestic savings to fund growth: many Balkan holders of European currencies exchanged them for euros through the banks to avoid conversion fees that otherwise would have applied. It would appear that distrust of the banks remains high, as much of this money did not remain on deposit.

Throughout the region, some leaders already have made the tough but vital decision to liquidate nonviable banks, usually the largest, and to rehabilitate and sell the remaining few to more qualified and better capitalized foreign or domestic owners.[39] In Serbia, for example, four of the major banks were closed in January 2002, and their assets will be liquidated at auction. Another nineteen smaller banks have been closed. Five reputable foreign banks from countries that are important trading partners have been licensed to operate new banks.

---

[39] In Kosovo, the EU has set up the Banking and Payments Authority of Kosovo (BPK). Largely staffed by foreigners, the BPK functions as Kosovo's central bank, issuing licenses to banks and supervising them as well. The five banks licensed to operate have attracted a strong deposit base and are potentially positioned to remedy the current scarcity of credit available to private sector entrepreneurs.

Nevertheless, the reform process remains unfinished. In Macedonia, local banks have been sold to foreign banks that are restoring their financial condition and upgrading their services, yet credit is still scarce, and creditworthy borrowers who can operate successfully in the precarious business environment are in short supply. Privatization and closure have reduced the number of banks in Bosnia to 35 (from 55) and to 18 in Republika Srpska—a number that could shrink further as more banks are put under provisional administration. But the population lacks confidence in the local banks, and the few foreign banks doing business in Bosnia now control 70 percent of the total banking assets in the country. This lack of confidence is a major force restraining credit growth. Again, the challenge is for savings kept "under the mattress" to be deposited in banks so that the money can be mobilized to finance small businesses and private industry and create jobs. This will only happen when citizens are convinced that banks can be trusted—that is, when banks are better capitalized and better managed.

Virtually all existing bad bank loans are debts owed by insolvent state enterprises. These enterprises need to be restructured in parallel with bank reform. Restructuring and privatizing state-owned enterprises is crucial to economic recovery. When conducted in a transparent and proper manner, it brings in much-needed capital investment, creates economically efficient companies, and positively affects levels of growth and productivity in the economy. Privatization also removes any improper ties formed between banks and state-owned enterprises (hence the bad bank loans), as well as other forms of corruption.

However, restructuring and privatizing public sector enterprises has serious social ramifications and is politically difficult. As dinosaur industries are streamlined or closed, subsidies are reduced, jobs are lost, and prices rise.[40] The collapse of large publicly owned enterprises can also mean the end of health care, pensions, and other essential local public services—a gap that private investors cannot be expected to fill. Without infusions of aid to

---

[40] For example, in the Serbian town of Kragujevac, home to the giant auto producer Zastava, 14,000 of the enterprise's 30,000 employees have been laid off.

Appendixes

soften the economic and social effects of privatization, political backlash is likely.

The Task Force therefore recommends that an important priority of the international donor community be well-funded programs to mitigate the social impact of economic decisions of reform governments. It is also imperative that national and local leaders devise strategies to address the lack of municipal services that may result from privatization. The World Bank and, potentially, the EBRD can provide funding for these projects.

Enterprise restructuring and privatization is underway in Serbia, Macedonia, and Bosnia. In Serbia, within six months of the passage of a privatization law (written with strong support from the World Bank and enacted in 2001), three cement factories were sold to foreign companies. More than forty other companies are being prepared for sale under international tender procedures that allow the sale of at least 70 percent of equity to strategic investors. Although there has been some domestic criticism of the allegedly low prices at which the cement factories were sold, the Serbian government has stated that its goal is not to raise the most money, but to attract investment from financially sound foreign companies with strong technology and research-and-development capabilities.[41] Restructuring of commercially viable (but currently money-losing) publicly owned enterprises to prepare them for privatization has begun with Zastava, the giant auto producer in Kragujevac. Enterprises in ten more company towns are being addressed in 2002.

In Macedonia, the World Bank is overseeing a program of enterprise restructuring that involves closing more than 40 money-losing enterprises—a program that has placed immediate pressure on the government, since the private sector has not developed enough to offer alternative employment. The results are also mixed in Bosnia, where privatization has increased but has not succeeded in improving the quality of management or increasing access to the financial resources required to fund growth.

---

[41] This effort is beginning to pay dividends; for example, in March 2002, U.S. Steel made a significant investment in SARTID, a Serbian steel plant.

One place where privatization is not proceeding is Kosovo. Normally the West would encourage the privatizing of state assets, but the UN is resisting because Kosovo's indeterminate status raises fundamental questions about who should receive the economic benefits of the assets. However thorny these issues are, they need not be impediments to proceeding with privatization, as they pale in comparison to the problems that will develop if pervasive unemployment persists. Kosovo needs jobs and the best—indeed, the only—way to create enough of them is to encourage development of the private sector.

The UN Mission in Kosovo (UNMIK) would do well to legally facilitate some privatization. UNMIK has full authority under Resolution 1244 to institute a privatization program for state and publicly owned assets. Purchasers of such assets should receive clear title, freeing those assets for further investment and productive use. The proceeds of these sales should be placed in escrow pending the resolution of status issues, and then should be released in accordance with the outcome of neutral arbitral proceedings. UNMIK should also allow citizens to secure title to private property. Already UNMIK has started registering and issuing license plates for the vehicles that clog Kosovo's roads. UNMIK has also registered more than 40,000 businesses in Kosovo that are now submitting to external audit and paying taxes to UNMIK's Central Fiscal Authority. The international community would do well to encourage more of these registration, licensing, taxing, and enforcement functions to devolve to Kosovar institutions, and then hold them accountable for transparency and performance.

With job creation such an urgent political need in Kosovo and throughout the region, and with little prospect that existing industry will create more jobs, the international community must be creative in providing multifaceted support for small and medium-sized private business development. Skills programs, business training, foreign education and internship programs, and special credit lines for new businesses all can do much to prepare citizens for the new market challenges their economies face.[42] The World Bank, the Southeast Europe Enterprise Development (SEED) initiative, and the EBRD are likely funding sources for such programs.

Increasing investment is only part of the puzzle; increasing trade, both regionally and between the Balkans and Europe, is also necessary. Doing so requires that trade and customs procedures in Balkan countries be liberalized in line with EU standards and policies; and that an intraregional network of compatible bilateral trade agreements be created.[43] Both are priorities in the EU's Stabilization and Association Process, and the EU can set the conditions and/or provide the technical and legal assistance for their completion.

The poor state of the region's physical infrastructure is an impediment to both trade and investment in the region. The reconstruction of roads, bridges, and power plants is required, and should be funded, at least initially, by the EIB and organizations such as the European Agency for Reconstruction (EAR).[44] Once the credit rating of the country improves, other private sector and/or public-private sector alternatives may become available with the assistance of risk-mitigation programs offered by multilateral banks and export credit agencies.

Finally, experience elsewhere in central and eastern Europe has demonstrated that financial reform strategy has to be synchronized with parallel steps in other parts of political society. Reform of the judicial system and an overhaul of financial sector legislation are linked to successful financial sector reform, which itself is necessary to encourage trade and investment. The integrity of the

---

[42] Creation of mortgage finance systems to promote housing finance and labor mobility—a function that, in most modern countries, has been assumed by privately owned savings banks, sometimes with government backing—would also aid investment.

[43] Under the Stability Pact, numerous bilateral free trade agreements are either in place or in negotiation: for example, between Yugoslavia and Bosnia, Yugoslavia and Croatia, and Yugoslavia and Hungary; between Croatia and Hungary and Croatia and Bosnia; and between Macedonia and Bosnia and Macedonia and Albania.

[44] The 2004 Summer Olympic Games in Athens provide a particular incentive to improve roads and other infrastructure linking Serbia and Greece, in the process adding a needed boost to intraregional and European trade and tourism.

financial system and the independence of financial supervision from affected parties and political interests needs to be guaranteed and enforced by law, with the rights and remedies of investors and creditors being non-negotiable. The treatment of commercial disputes and property rights requires codification. Taxation needs to be simplified and rationalized so that it is reasonable to comply. Reform of labor market legislation and of the administrative barriers to foreign and direct investment is also necessary. So far, efforts to bring about these reforms have been insufficient, threatening the success of the entire economic transition.

III. OTHER ECONOMIC ISSUES IN THE BALKANS

The recommendations listed above apply to all the Balkan states, except Slovenia and Croatia. Serbia and Bosnia face additional challenges to their economic reform efforts that deserve special mention.

After Milosevic's downfall, the new Serbian government was shocked at the severity of the country's economic deterioration. Per capita gross domestic product (GDP) stood below $1,000, a 60 percent drop from the level a decade earlier. External debt totaled $11.4 billion, more than 140 percent of GDP. Unemployment was close to 50 percent, the average wage was about $40 per month, and the inflation rate hovered at 112 percent. A strict program of macroeconomic stabilization, coupled with fiscal reform and the liberalization of prices and tariffs, has achieved remarkable results in a short time. Inflation is down, GDP is growing, and unemployment is decreasing. The dinar is stable and convertible. Reserves, which a year ago were $200 million, are now at $1.3 billion—equivalent to 2.5 months of imports. Yugoslavia has settled its arrears with the IMF, the World Bank, and the EIB, paving the way for new borrowing relationships. The Paris Club has agreed to reduce Yugoslavia's debt by 66 percent, and similar terms are expected from other international creditors. All but six major taxes have been eliminated and those that remain have been simplified. In short, the economic and financial policies of the government of Serbia deserve strong international support, for they are creating the basis for a sustainable economy, one that could be the engine for growth throughout the Balkans.[45]

However, to restore its important borrowing relationship with the World Bank, Yugoslavia had to repay its past-due loans— including those incurred by Kosovo, which, until the resolution of its status, remains legally a part of Yugoslavia. Since Serbia does not control Kosovo politically or economically, Serbia's economic leaders think it is unreasonable to hold Serbia accountable for repayment of Kosovo's debts. In Kosovo, the United Nations is collecting customs duties and tax revenue under the powers granted to it by Security Council Resolution 1244. However, neither Kosovo nor the United Nations will discuss the issue of repayment of Kosovo's share of the World Bank obligations with Serbia, claiming instead that this issue does not fall under the purview of Resolution 1244.

The Task Force recommends that the international community consider suspending payments on Kosovo's share of the World Bank debt until there is final agreement on Kosovo's status. The disposition of the Kosovo debt could then be decided in the proper political context and perhaps be used as a powerful inducement for agreement in final status talks.

The case of Bosnia is particularly troubling for the international community. True economic integration in Bosnia is thwarted by conflicting political structures that are often manipulated for ethnic or nationalist purposes. Economic recovery, which started out strong in 1996 following the end of the war, is tapering off as international aid declines. The current GDP estimate is $4.3 billion (about $1,000 per capita), up from $1.5 billion in 1994, but still less than half the estimated $8.7 billion in 1991 (about $2,000 per capita). Inflation has stabilized at about 5 percent and does not appear to pose any threat in the near term.

---

[45] The March 2002 status agreement between Serbia and Montenegro will add a new dimension to economic reform and activity in both places. The agreement provides for two currencies, two markets, two tariff and customs systems, and two sets of institutions, but a common representative to the international financial institutions and international organizations. It is unclear what effect this agreement will have.

Bosnia is hampered by its multilayered governmental structure and by the same factors found in the other Balkan countries: an inefficient public sector, organized crime, an inadequate legal system, a poorly functioning banking and financial intermediation system, and increasing dependence on international assistance. Massive inefficiencies and corruption haunt the economy, despite good progress on regulatory reforms.

Revenue collection is a major challenge for the government. The Bosnian central government rules are applied selectively by Republika Srpska, if not ignored. Smuggling and corruption have cut public receipts by as much as half. A survey by the World Bank showed a major mistrust of government by private citizens and public officials, who regard the tax, customs, and court systems, the police, and managers of public enterprises as highly corrupt. Clearly this is not a solid foundation upon which to build a competitive, 21st–century economy capable of entering the European Union within a decade.

Bosnia badly needs sensible, countrywide economic management rather than ethnic-based, politically driven decisions with dubious economic merit at the entity or canton level. This will involve consolidating duplicative functions at the entity and canton level so that there is one customs authority, one fiscal authority, one central bank, a national payments system, and one banking regulatory agency for all of Bosnia. The Task Force recommends that the Office of the High Representative (OHR) and the Economic Task Force make the creation of a single economic space in Bosnia its top economic priority.

APPENDIX D: REFUGEES AND INTERNALLY DISPLACED PEOPLE

I. INTRODUCTION

Refugees and people displaced within their own countries are the living symbols of the unfinished business from the conflicts in the Balkans. Their return to their homes, or resettlement in new communities if they prefer, is essential to a sustainable peace.

Both the 1995 Dayton Peace Agreement for Bosnia and UN Security Council Resolution 1244, adopted after the 1999 Kosovo conflict, guarantee refugees and internally displaced persons the right to return home. Yet there are more than 1.2 million refugees and displaced people in the shattered pieces of Tito's Yugoslavia. More than 900,000 are from Bosnia and Herzegovina, Croatia, and the Federal Republic of Yugoslavia (excluding Kosovo), even though armed conflict in those countries ended more than six years ago. Another 250,000 are from Kosovo, many of whom will not return because of the role they played there under the Milosevic regime; because economic opportunities are limited, particularly for non-Albanian speakers; and because security for non-Albanians in Kosovo is still inadequate. Conflict in the border region between southern Serbia and Macedonia forced as many as 150,000 people to flee their villages in 2000. At the beginning of 2002, more than 40,000 people remained displaced in that area, mostly from Macedonia.

Nevertheless, 2001 was an encouraging year. In Bosnia, 92,000 members of minority populations returned to their municipalities of origin. This figure was much higher than the one from the previous year, which in turn was significantly higher than the returns in 1999. The increases are attributable to several factors, including more effective implementation of property laws, greater commitment by local authorities, better security, and improved freedom of movement.

Protecting the right of refugees to return and ensuring their safety remains central to the goal of tolerant societies in the Balkans. Nevertheless, it is clear that many refugees and internally displaced people, especially Serbs, do not want to go back to their communities of origin; they would rather resettle in Serbia than go back to Croatia, Bosnia, or Kosovo.[46] This means that resolving the refugee problem will require permanent resettlement, as well as continuing returns.

It is incumbent upon all governments and international agencies to accept and defend the right of refugees to return if they wish. At the same time, governments and international agencies must recognize that some individuals and families may choose resettlement over repatriation; those governments and agencies need to provide reasonable support for those who make this choice. The Task Force recommends a clear policy stand by the European Union, supporting the right of refugees to return or resettle within the Balkan region and even elsewhere. So far there have been barriers to resettlement—especially in Serbia—that prevented Serb refugees from Croatia, Bosnia, and Kosovo from resettling in Serbia. The new democratic regime in Belgrade has dropped this policy and deserves assistance for its resettlement efforts. The EU should take the lead and the UN High Commissioner for Refugees (UNHCR), aid donors, and other relief agencies should support the EU's efforts in this regard. As people are resettled, they can become productive and be removed from the refugee assistance rolls.

Despite the consolidation of ethnic populations caused by resettlement, especially among Serbs, members of minority groups have returned in sufficient numbers throughout the Balkans (Kosovo being a major exception) to begin creating some stable and expanding ethnic integration, particularly if countries and agen-

---

[46] A survey conducted by the UNHCR in 2001 found that 60 percent of the more than 390,000 refugees in Yugoslavia wish to remain where they are, while only 5 percent want to return home. In Serbia, the majority of refugees who participated in a recent re-registration exercise—mostly ethnic Serbs from Bosnia and Kosovo—said they preferred to remain in Serbia and integrate with the local population. The new government of Serbia is encouraging this trend, the main impediments to which are economic. United Nations High Commissioner for Refugees, *Refugee Registration in Serbia* (Belgrade: June 18, 2001).

cies continue to improve law enforcement and economic protections. The removal of leaders who stoked conflict through ethnic demagoguery has improved the atmosphere regionwide. Yet the hope for a society with at least pockets of ethnic variety will be realized only by *making* it work, not by hoping it will work.

While some issues affecting refugees are purely local, others—such as property rights, citizenship, and pension rights—require regional solutions. The Task Force recommends that the European Union establish a regionwide working group to expedite coherent solutions to the issues of property rights and compensation, pensions, citizenship, and health care. This group would consist of representatives from all concerned governments, the UNHCR, NATO, the OHR, UNMIK, international agencies, and major NGOs, and could begin working by the end of 2003. Toward this end, the Task Force is encouraged that Yugoslavia's national strategy for refugees calls for "information sharing mechanisms to be put in place between Serbia, Croatia, and Bosnia and Herzegovina in order to: facilitate planning at the national level, monitor refugee movements, and avoid abuses of refugee status."[47] This initiative could form the basis for cross-border cooperation and planning critical to resolving many of the problems facing the displaced in the region.

Returning refugees to their homes and integrating those who wish to stay where they are are tasks the international community can achieve well before 2010. Significant returns have been taking place since 1995, and the pace, particularly into Bosnia, has accelerated. However, if the overall displacement problem is to be solved on a permanent basis, important challenges remain. These need to be addressed simultaneously and continuously until at least 2005, and in many instances beyond. The challenges include restitution of property, security, housing and employment assistance, and long-term sustainability.

---

[47] Federal Republic of Yugoslavia, "National Strategy for Resolving the Problems of Refugees, Expellees, and Displaced Persons" (Draft of September 28, 2001), p. 14.

II. RESTITUTION OF PROPERTY

An essential condition for the return of refugees is guarantees for property rights.[48]

The most encouraging development for refugees is the recognition that the right to property is a basic human right. It is confirmed in Bosnian law, as well as in Serbia's National Strategy for Resolving the Problems of Refugees, Expellees, and Displaced Persons. Establishing property rights requires that an acceptable legal framework and a procedural mechanism for restitution or compensation be devised to handle property claims. That facilitates refugee return, resettlement, and integration into new communities.

Sorting out property rights remains the most vexatious and time-consuming aspect of arranging returns.[49] Yet it is essential for both returns and resettlement. As the Yugoslav National Strategy notes, a much sounder basis for refugees' integration would be created by permission to sell private property, compensation for loss of tenancy rights, pension benefits, and the right to participate in the privatization process.[50]

According to anecdotal information, an unknown but significant number of Serbs who fled Kosovo have sold their property there, securing a nest egg for reinvestment in Serbia. Accounts of Kosovar Albanians seeking out Serbs displaced to Serbia and

---

[48] The establishment and protection of property rights are also key preconditions for private investment.

[49] This is particularly true in Croatia, where progress on this issue has been slow. Of the 250,000 Serbs who fled or were expelled from Croatia during the 1991–1995 conflict, approximately 100,000 have returned. However, while legal procedures have been adopted for Serbs wanting to have their citizenship recognized, to obtain documentation, and to reclaim their property, implementation and enforcement have been uneven. Some Serbs have been arrested upon return to Croatia, in violation of procedures agreed to with the UNHCR. Repatriated Serbs often find their residences occupied and encounter difficulty with the restitution of occupied properties. Despite the establishment of a legal commission to facilitate minority returns, there has been little progress in rectifying cases of illegal occupancy—even when a court decision has established the rights of the original tenant (usually a Serb). The Council of Europe reports that Croatia has not fully abolished discriminatory laws regulating refugee returns.

[50] Government of the Republic of Serbia, "National Strategy for Resolving the Problems of Refugees and Internally Displaced Persons" (Draft of May 30, 2002), p. 16.

offering to buy the property they left behind are quite common. Serbs who sell have no intention of returning to Kosovo.

Currently the ability of local authorities to implement property laws is weak. Judicial and law enforcement personnel require instruction on property rights issues as part of the training they receive from international donors, including the EU, and incentives, such as local development funds, to enforce the law scrupulously.

III. SECURITY

A second essential condition for return is the protection of individuals.

While security has improved throughout the region, there are still tensions in some hard-line communities, especially in Kosovo. By December 2001, only 2,432 Serbs had returned, out of 229,900 displaced from Kosovo during the 1999 NATO bombing campaign and subsequent Albanian uprising. Two-thirds of those returns occurred in 2000; the pace actually slowed in 2001. Lack of security is an important barrier to Serb returns. Without a dramatic change of circumstances there, the number able or willing to return is likely to be modest, at least in the short term.

Refugees returning to Bosnia faced similar challenges in the early stages. Only when SFOR became fully involved in the process in 1997 did returns improve. Now nearly 400,000 refugees have returned, and minority returns have risen significantly in the last few years. The lesson for Kosovo is obvious: returns will not occur without security assistance.

The Task Force therefore recommends that both UNMIK and KFOR pursue the return issue aggressively. Experience in Bosnia after 1997 can provide guidelines for action.

Though continuation of the NATO missions in Bosnia, Kosovo, and Macedonia is essential, local authorities are still responsible for providing a safe and secure environment for all inhabitants. Throughout the region, refugees and the internally displaced face a dismaying catalogue of problems that go far beyond personal security and freedom of movement. The most serious are loss of homes, farms, and livelihood; loss of job eligibility and opportunity; lack of citizenship rights; the psychological trauma of flight; ethnic discrimination in education, health care, and other social services; and denial of access to basic services such as electricity, gas, and telephones. Some recently adopted laws have stipulated that refugees are entitled to temporary accommodation, health care, food, and education, but too many local authorities have been reluctant to provide these basic rights. The Task Force thus recommends a concerted strategy to ensure that the treatment of refugees and the displaced meets human rights standards.

IV. ASSISTANCE

Continued funding for refugee returns—including international assistance for housing reconstruction, employment programs, and the protection of refugees once they return home—is crucial. The biggest threat to successful return and resettlement in the region is a decline of funding for integration programs. Refugees who have returned to Bosnia continue to live in tents next to their destroyed houses, because reconstruction aid has not kept pace with needs. To facilitate both return and resettlement, donors have to continue to provide adequate levels of funding through the EU and the UNHCR.

The severe shortage of housing for refugees and the displaced is a top priority for international donors. In some places, legal and bureaucratic obstacles add further complications. In Bosnia, for example, a well-intentioned regulation imposed by the Office of the High Representative requires that a house found more than 60 percent destroyed must be demolished and replaced rather than repaired. But the majority of the owners of houses in this category are the least able to afford the cost of rebuilding, and funding shortages remain. The hard reality is that many new houses must be built throughout the region. This is a humanitarian issue with political and security implications. Failure to address the housing problem will be exploited by demagogues and eventually lead to political disaffection and a return to instability.

V. INTEGRATION

Refugees are returning now to areas where the economy barely functions. Other refugees are resettling in areas that are unable to support the additional population in jobs or services. Economic revival is critical for peace and reconciliation; lack of economic opportunity could overwhelm whatever fragile goodwill has been established in the return process.

The Task Force recommends the inclusion of refugees and displaced persons in the plans for bilateral and multilateral initiatives to alleviate poverty and stimulate development (including employment programs and small-business loans and grants). Agricultural investment and supports require special attention. Such moves will be essential for the success of local integration plans.

Some steps have already been taken to facilitate integration in Serbia. Indeed, efforts are now underway to move refugees into their own housing and farms. Furthermore, a law allowing refugees to become Yugoslav citizens while retaining their current citizenship was implemented in 2001. This dual citizenship law facilitates property ownership and removes legal barriers to job eligibility, and the Task Force urges other regional governments to adopt similar legislation by 2003.

APPENDIX E: IDENTITY, CIVIL SOCIETY, AND THE MEDIA

I. CIVIL SOCIETY AND THE ROLE OF NONGOVERNMENTAL ORGANIZATIONS

The disintegration of the former Yugoslavia in the 1990s had deep, tragic consequences. Violence disrupted communities. Old systems of government and economic management collapsed before new ones could be installed. The social safety net unraveled. But poorer and less educated social groups—which in many communities meant the majority of the population—retained their mentality of dependence on the state, nurturing the illusion that the state, or political parties and leaders, would take care of everything, and that citizens, individually and collectively, are powerless to bring about real change. This attitude has persisted and severely inhibits the development of a strong, independent civil society.

There is little history of civic action in the Balkans on issues on which NGOs are active and influential in the West, such as environmental protection or advocacy for disadvantaged groups. Those civic entities that did exist during the Communist era were marginalized and persecuted by the state. While some organizations of civil society in Serbia—such as the youth movement OTPOR, G-17/G-17 Plus, the Center for Free Elections and Democracy (CESID), the Association of Independent Electronic Media, and the radio station B92—were crucial in engineering the ouster of Slobodan Milosevic in 2000, they lack the tools today to build on their success. Elsewhere in the region civil society is even weaker, especially in rural areas.[51]

---

[51] In Bosnia and Herzegovina, for example, government is fragmented, corruption is endemic, and the rule of law is more aspiration than fact. It is unsurprising that civil society is not thriving—especially in Republika Srpska, where dire economic circumstances, opposition to the idea of a unified Bosnian state, and deep distrust of international organizations make it hard to develop and support civic action.

However, organizations of civil society—NGOs, watchdog groups, charities, religious organizations, and above all independent media—are working for the first time with Balkan governments on economic, political, and legal reform. These activities are potentially fertile ground for nascent civic organizations in the Balkans that want to expand their role in public life.

With the support of think tanks and public opinion researchers, NGOs can bolster the democratic process by providing mechanisms for citizen participation in government decision-making and by strengthening cooperation with public administrators. They can make government institutions accountable and can have a constructive voice in the formulation of government policies.

While it is essential for NGOs to work closely with government, it is also essential for them to retain their independence and freedom to dissent publicly as part of a constructive dialogue. To do so, these organizations need to become financially self-sustaining.

At present, civil society organizations are almost entirely dependent on foreign contributions, which limits both their resources and the number of citizens with a stake in their success. In order to rectify this, legislatures will first have to enact measures granting legal status to NGOs and nonprofit groups, which at present have no statutory terms for establishing a legal identity. Governments then need to grant tax-exempt status to not-for-profit organizations, with the provision that individuals that contribute to such organizations may deduct the gifts from their taxes (as is done in the United States). A further step in the right direction would be the granting to NGOs of discounts, refunds, or exemptions from other taxes, such as customs duties or the value-added tax.[52] The passage, by all the national legislatures of the region, of statutes granting legal identity and tax benefits to nonprofit or nongovernmental groups is key to the development of the civil society sector and can be completed by 2004.

Adoption of such measures would boost philanthropy, legitimize the value of charitable practices, and greatly improve the confi-

---

[52] This is not a unanimous recommendation of the Task Force; some members note that enacting such measures in transition countries can lead to abuse and difficulty in enforcing the tax code.

dence of civil society activists. The loss of tax revenue is easily justified, even in these relatively poor countries, by the fact that these organizations would perform socially valuable tasks without relying on the state. However, even if tax-exempt status was enacted into law, NGOs would not benefit in the short term, since there is little tradition of charitable giving in these countries. This raises the requirement that Western NGOs and volunteer organizations active in the Balkans train their local counterparts in fund-raising techniques.

II. EDUCATION AND BALKAN NATIONALISM

Education reform is another key to the future of a tolerant, vibrant civil society in the Balkans. According to a 2001 UN High Commissioner for Refugees (UNHCR) report, school curricula continue to be dominated by nationalist ideology, and minority returnees are often denied access to educational facilities. This situation simultaneously discourages the return of minority families and encourages brain drain among the local population.[53] Identifying, supporting, and extending positive examples in education—curricula, texts, and teaching approaches—are top priorities.

Some European governments, especially that of Austria, are bringing together governments, NGOs, and donors to support education reform in Serbia, Croatia, and Kosovo. This effort deserves to be expanded. In particular, the European Commission and European bilateral donors can earmark money for education and for the Education Network in the region.

International civil society organizations are also leading a push to overcome curriculum bias and revise textbooks. The Open Society Institute, Croatia, is sponsoring a project furthering cooperation between educational institutions and experts from the region. The Center for Democracy and Reconciliation in Southeast Europe, based in Thessalonike, has undertaken a project to

---

[53] Local surveys in Bosnia suggest that by adolescence, more than half of local youths seek a future outside the country.

review and revise history textbooks. Expunging outdated doctrines and nationalist ideology from the classroom can be completed by the end of the decade. EU and American funding for education programs in the region require conditionality in order to ensure progress by local authorities in this important effort.

III. THE MEDIA

The development of a free and responsible press is fundamental for reasoned debate about public issues and the levying of accountability on governments and political parties. It is therefore essential that the European Union and other donors—along with international NGOs and media watchdog groups—increase pressure on Balkan governments to enact the needed media reforms.

A necessary first step is the transformation of the state-run media. State-run media outlets can either be privatized through competitive bidding or converted into public service organizations. One model is the experience of countries in eastern and central Europe that converted their state-run media outlets. This requirement can be enforced by the European Union as part of its Stabilization and Association Process.

Privatizing local and regional radio and television stations allows market forces to drive media competition. This is especially important in Serbia, where media organizations are caught up in the political battle between Prime Minister Zoran Djindjic and President Vojislav Kostunica. However, similar steps need to be taken in other Balkan countries, again with EU assistance and stimulated by EU standards.

Responsibility for developing independent and reliable media does not rest entirely with the government. International media organizations and journalists can help by working with local organizations and NGOs. The Network for the Professionalization of Media, which includes 17 media training institutions in 11 countries, has begun training Serbian journalists in the standards and techniques of their profession. The Task Force urges that such efforts be expanded. In particular, the Task Force recommends that

European and American media organizations, such as the International Center for Journalists, include more Balkan journalists in exchange programs so that they might observe the workings of the press in free societies. In addition to the exchange component, there is a need for in-country training on specific topics, such as reporting economic and agricultural news.

Freedom to publish is not the same as freedom to be irresponsible. It is understandable that newly liberated news organizations wish to be free of censorship or government control, but some of these organizations have not yet understood their obligation to be accurate and impartial. The Task Force recommends that journalists and editors adopt a voluntary code of conduct—which any of several international NGOs could help them draft—to police themselves in this new environment. Penalties for deviating from the code, if any, are properly set and enforced by journalists and publishers, not by any state entity. The Association of Electronic Independent Media and the Independent Association of Journalists of Serbia are reworking their codes. Political divisions among journalists have so far impeded the adoption of a code.

Some Balkan nations are doing better in media reform than others, but nowhere are the stakes higher than in Serbia, which was responsible for much of the region's conflict in the past decade. The accession to power of the coalition known as the Democratic Opposition of Serbia (DOS) presented an opportunity for the Serbian media to liberate itself from the constraints of the Milosevic era. But so far the pace of media reform has lagged far behind the expectations of the public—and of journalists. According to Veran Matic, editor in chief of Radio-TV B92, one of the most respected independent media outlets in Serbia,

> More substantial changes in the system have bypassed the media. Of even more concern is the suspicion that the utter lack of any change in the media sector is not due to some combination of unfortunate circumstances but to the conscious determination of the people now wielding political power to retain certain mechanisms formerly used by the Milosevic regime to exert pressure on the media.[54]

---

[54] From a Task Force discussion with Mr. Matic, February 2002.

The DOS government's initial media reforms were laudable. The Serbian Ministry of Information, one of the instruments by which the Milosevic regime suppressed the media, was abolished. The 1998 Serbian Public Information Act, used to control media that did not conform to government policies, was repealed. And fines levied against journalists and their organization under the information act were returned.

But the passage of a Public Broadcasting Bill, which will set broadcasting standards and a process for granting broadcast licenses, has long been delayed. Its companion bill, the Public Information Act, designed to protect the freedoms of an independent media, is stalled in the Serbian parliament. The slow pace of media reform gives the impression that the DOS government wanted to maintain control over the press, especially because the government managed to push through other measures, but not these. Prime Minister Djindjic, blamed by reform advocates for delays, even disparaged the media reform measures as extra "privileges."

A moratorium on broadcasting licenses remains in place. Independent media outlets, such as B92, continue to operate without licenses and run the risk of legal sanctions, while broadcast outlets that were sympathetic to Milosevic retain their privileges.

The state-run media outlets, such as Radio Television Serbia and Tanjug News Service, have switched their allegiance to the DOS-led government, which has yet to announce a plan to transform state-run media outlets into public service broadcasters or privately operated entities.

In addition to the necessary transformation or privatization of the state-run media, the Task Force recommends the passage and full implementation of the draft law that guarantees the independence of the Serbian media. The Serbian government also needs to audit the state and private media outlets that profited during the Milosevic era through tax breaks or government kickbacks. Recovered funds could be used to support public service broadcasting, as with the BBC, which receives public money but is independent of government control.

APPENDIX F: STAKEHOLDERS IN THE BALKANS— GOVERNMENTS, SUPRANATIONAL AND INTERNATIONAL ORGANIZATIONS, NONGOVERNMENTAL ORGANIZATIONS, AND THE BUSINESS COMMUNITY

Perhaps more than any other region in Europe in the last decade, the Balkans has been the focus of significant external interest, financial aid, humanitarian relief, and development assistance. This aid and assistance has come from governments across Europe, and from the United States and Japan; from supranational and international organizations such as the United Nations, the European Union, and their various agencies; from international financial institutions such as the World Bank; and from nongovernmental organizations and grant-making foundations. In recent years, European and American businesses have also started to take notice of the Balkans. Given the privatization programs being conducted in Serbia, Bosnia, and Croatia, the cheap labor force, and abundant natural resources, the region is rich with investment opportunities; continued improvement of transport links and infrastructure rehabilitation will further attract foreign and domestic investment.

This appendix aims to clarify who the major stakeholders in the region are, what they are doing, and how much they are spending.

GOVERNMENTS AND BILATERAL ASSISTANCE

In addition to aid and assistance funneled to the region through international and supranational organizations and the international financial institutions, many European countries, and the United States and Japan, conduct separate bilateral assistance programs with the countries of the region. Apart from this financial and in-kind assistance, of course, the United States and European nations

exert political, economic, and social influence over the Balkan countries; for example, the U.S. use of conditionality with the Federal Republic of Yugoslavia is commonly credited with causing the
handover of Slobodan Milosevic to The Hague tribunal in June
2001. Some of the most significant external governmental players in the region are:

- **The United States:** U.S. aid and development assistance to the
  region is primarily channeled through the U.S. Agency for International Development (USAID), and takes the form of infrastructure reconstruction, economic and private sector development
  programs, and democracy and civil society–building programs.
  Between FY 1999 and FY 2002, USAID funding to Bosnia,
  Croatia, Kosovo, Macedonia, Montenegro, and Serbia exceed-
  ed $1.8 billion. Funding levels peaked in FY 2001, and fund-
  ing priorities have shifted over time, with assistance to Bosnia
  decreasing annually since 1996 and funding to Croatia and
  Yugoslavia leapfrogging over Bosnian aid after political changes
  in 2000. For more information on USAID activities in eastern
  Europe, see http://www.usaid.gov/regions/europe_eurasia/;
  for statistics, including per-country allocations, see
  http://www.usaid.gov/pubs/cbj2002/tablexp.html.

- **Germany:** For the period 2000–2003, Germany has committed a total of €614 million ($607 million) for Stability Pact
  purposes. Germany also disburses smaller amounts annually as
  part of its regular bilateral development cooperation with
  southeast Europe and is a main bilateral donor in Kosovo. German aid money is disbursed through the Federal Foreign
  Office and the Federal Ministry for Economic Cooperation
  and Development; for more information, see http://www.
  auswaertiges-amt.de/www/en/index.html and http://www.bmz.de/
  en/index.html.

- **United Kingdom:** The United Kingdom has pledged £115
  million ($179 million) for technical assistance under the aus-
  pices of the Stability Pact for the years 2000–2003 and, in addition, has committed £24.5 million ($38.3 million) for a U.K.-led

Conflict Prevention Initiative in the region for 2001–2004. The U.K. contributes approximately 17.5 percent of all EU aid in the region. See http://www.fco.gov.uk.

- **Italy:** In addition to its contributions to the EU aid budget, Italy has set aside approximately €196 million ($194 million) for bilateral initiatives and soft loans to Balkan countries for the years 2001–2003. Italy has also committed over €115 million ($114 million) to Serbia and Montenegro's reconstruction, the most of any individual donor. See information on its Balkans Task Force at http://www.esteri.it/eng/foreignpol/index.htm.

- **Greece:** Separate from the EU aid policy to the region, Greece is implementing a Hellenic Plan for Economic Reconstruction of the Balkans, with a provisional budget of €550 million ($544 million), and is also active in facilitating trade and investment incentives and infrastructure rehabilitation in the region; for more information, see http://www.greekembassy.org/politics/balkans.

- **Japan:** Despite focusing most of its external aid and development assistance in east and southwest Asia, Japan contributed almost $31 million in grant aid to Bosnia, Yugoslavia (including Kosovo), and Macedonia in fiscal year 2001, and has pledged to continue to provide assistance for economic, environmental, and infrastructure development and humanitarian relief as needed. See http://www.mofa.go.jp/policy/oda/index.html.

Information about Balkan governments themselves is now more readily available than in the past; indeed, the Balkan countries seem to be becoming increasingly sophisticated in their presentation and public relations, with most sporting slick websites that feature at least some content in English in addition to the local language or languages. The array of sites and available data—which, overall, is somewhat sparse and occasionally contradictory—testifies to the complicated governmental structures that prevail in some of the countries, such as Bosnia and Herzegovina and Serbia and Montenegro.

- **Bosnia and Herzegovina:** Bosnia's complex governmental structures, the supremacy of the two individual entities over the common institutions, and the lack of interentity cooperation are all demonstrated on the web. Both the Federation of Bosnia and Herzegovina and Republika Srpska governments have adequate, if not extensive, sites, but there is no central site for the common (state) institutions; information is decentralized and dispersed, and neither entity has links to the other entity on its main site. For the government of the Federation of Bosnia and Herzegovina, see http://www.fbihvlada.gov.ba/ engleski/index.html; for Republika Srpska, see http:// www.vladars.net/en/. Each page features information on the respective governments and links to entity-level institutions. Two of the state-level institutions with a web presence are the Ministry of Foreign Affairs for Bosnia and Herzegovina, which administers Bosnia's foreign policy (see http://www.mvp.gov.ba/Index_eng.htm), and the Central Bank, which controls the implementation of monetary policy in BiH (http://www.cbbh.gov.ba/en/index.html).

- **Croatia:** The Croatian government has a central site with links to pages for specific offices and ministries, along with basic country information, current news, and links to important documents. The main site is found at http://www.vlada.hr/ english/about-government.html; for the Ministry of Economy, which oversees trade policy, industry, privatization, and investment, see http://www.mingo.hr/english/index.htm; for the Ministry of Finance, which oversees monetary policy, customs, and taxation, see http://www.mfin.hr/mfinenooo.htm; and for the Ministry of Foreign Affairs, see http://www.mvp.hr/ mvprh-www-eng/index.html.

- **Federal Republic of Yugoslavia:** The government of the Federal Republic of Yugoslavia and the government of Serbia maintain separate sites, as does the Montenegrin government (but no English version). Each includes links to select ministry sites; the Serbian government site also contains news, information on topical issues (such as Kosovo and the transition economy), and selected statistics. For the government of the Federal Republic of Yugoslavia, see http://www.gov.yu; for the federal Ministry of Foreign Affairs, see http://www.mfa.gov.yu/; for the Serbian government, see http://www.serbia.sr.gov.yu/; for the Serbian Ministry of Finance and Economy, see http://www.mfin.sr.gov.yu/html/index.php?newlang=eng; and for the Serbian Ministry of Economy and Privatization, see http://www.mpriv.sr.gov.yu/eng/default.asp.

- **Macedonia:** Macedonia's web presence ranges from bare bones (the government site, at http://www.gov.mk/English/index.htm) to useful and well documented (the Ministry of Defense site, which includes information on Macedonian cooperation with NATO and, in particular, the Partnership for Peace; see http://www.morm.gov.mk/). There are also sites for the Macedonian Assembly (http://www.assembly.gov.mk/Eng/beginning.htm), the presidency and cabinet (http://www.president.gov.mk/index_eng.htm), and the Finance Ministry, which includes information on tenders (http://www.finance.gov.mk/gb/index.html).

SUPRANATIONAL AND INTERNATIONAL ORGANIZATIONS

Many supranational and international organizations are engaged in varying degrees in the Balkans. Although each of the organizations and agencies has its own mandate and mission, generally speaking they are involved with providing reconstruction aid, humanitarian relief, and development assistance through civil society building, governance, rule of law, and private sector development programs. The European Union and the United Nations are the most prominent institutions in the region.

- **European Union:** The European Union is the single largest assistance donor to the western Balkans and—with the EU office in Kosovo and the European Agency for Reconstruction (EAR), an independent agency of the European Union operating in Serbia, Montenegro, Kosovo, and Macedonia—is expanding its field presence in the region. The European Investment Bank, which is involved with infrastructure financing in the Balkans, is also an EU agency (see below, "International Financial Institutions").

The cornerstone of the EU's involvement in the western Balkans—comprised of Bosnia and Herzegovina, Croatia, Serbia and Montenegro, Macedonia, and Albania—centers around its Stabilization and Association Process (SAP), which offers countries a strategy by which to achieve closer association with and integration into European structures. The SAP is both bilateral and regional, creating links between individual countries and the European Union and encouraging regional cooperation between the countries themselves. In conjunction with the Stabilization and Association Process the European Union operates an assistance program called Community Assistance for Reconstruction, Development, and Stabilization (CARDS), which provides financial support for the political, legal, and economic reforms and institution-building necessary to implement SAP obligations. For the period 2000–2006, approximately €4.65 billion ($4.6 billion) will be provided through the CARDS program in support of the SAP. In Yugoslavia (including Kosovo) and Macedonia, the European Agency for Reconstruction is responsible for the delivery of CARDS assistance. For more information on the SAP, see http://www.europa.eu.int/comm/external_relations/see/index.htm; for information on the European Agency for Reconstruction, see http://www.ear.eu.int. Some assistance also makes its way to the region outside of the CARDS scheme—for example, through the European Community Humanitarian Office (ECHO). However, the volume of aid given outside the SAP structure is decreasing. For information on ECHO, see http://europa.eu.int/comm/echo/en/index_en.html.

• **United Nations:** The most prominent UN agency in the region is the UN Mission in Kosovo. UNMIK, like the Office of the High Representative (OHR) in Bosnia, has direct policy responsibilities. Kosovo is essentially a UN protectorate, and many of its basic administrative and governmental functions are performed by UNMIK, in cooperation with the EU office in Kosovo and the Organization for Security and Cooperation in Europe (OSCE). For more information, see http://www. unmikonline.org. Other UN missions and agencies in the region include the UN Mission in Bosnia and Herzegovina (UNMIBH, http://www.unmibh.org), whose primary task is overseeing the International Police Task Force (IPTF) in Bosnia; the UN Development Program (UNDP), which operates in Albania, Bosnia, Croatia, Macedonia, and Yugoslavia (including Kosovo); the World Health Organization (WHO); the International Labor Organization (ILO); and the UN High Commissioner for Refugees (UNHCR).

- **Organization for Security and Cooperation in Europe:** The OSCE has active institution-building, election monitoring, democratization, and free media programs throughout the Balkans, with an especially strong presence in Kosovo, Macedonia (Skopje), and Bosnia. For FY 2002 the OSCE budgeted approximately €50.1 million ($49 million) for the OSCE mission in Kosovo; €21 million ($20.7 million) for the spillover monitor mission to Skopje; and €18.3 million ($18.1 million) for its ongoing mission to Bosnia, in addition to smaller disbursements to Yugoslavia and Croatia. For more information on the OSCE activities in southeast Europe, see http://www.osce.org/field_activities/.

- **Office of the High Representative in Bosnia and Herzegovina:** Like UNMIK, the Office of the High Representative has direct policy responsibilities. The OHR oversees the implementation of the civilian aspect of the Dayton Peace Agreement, and as such is authorized to impose legislation and dismiss obstructive officials. British politician Paddy Ashdown took over as high representative from Austrian Wolfgang Petritsch in May 2002. See http://www.ohr.int.

- **Council of Europe:** The Council of Europe (COE) is primarily active in the reconstruction and development efforts in southeast Europe through two channels: the Social Cohesion Initiative and the Council of Europe Development Bank. The former focuses on the application of human rights, access to health care, and other activities to support social development. The Council of Europe Development Bank, which defines itself as a multilateral bank with a social vocation, had disbursed over €300 million in the region by October 2001, in support of Stability Pact projects. For the Council of Europe Social Cohesion Initiative, see http://www.coe.int/T/E/ Social_Cohesion/; for the Council of Europe Development Bank, see http://www.coebank.org/homeen.htm.

- **Stability Pact:** The Stability Pact was created in 1999 to encourage respect for human and minority rights, conflict prevention, and the development of democratic institutions and market economies. It comprises more than 40 partner countries and organizations and is primarily useful in coordinating donors and mobilizing resources for the Balkans. It does not implement projects in the region but facilitates their implementation. For more information, including a comprehensive links page, see http://www.stabilitypact.org.

INTERNATIONAL FINANCIAL INSTITUTIONS

Alongside governments and international and supranational organizations, the international financial institutions are also engaged in the region. Of these, the World Bank is the most active.

- **Joint World Bank/European Commission Office on Southeast Europe:** This joint office acts as a clearinghouse for donor countries and organizations, by coordinating the projects in the region, developing strategies for regional development, providing needs assessments, and mobilizing support among donors. This office does not actually disburse loans, grants, or technical and development assistance, however; these are delivered through the World Bank office in the particular country. The World Bank now has offices in Albania, Bosnia and Herzegovina, Croatia, Macedonia, and Belgrade (for Serbia and Montenegro). For more information, see its comprehensive website at http://www.seerecon.org.

- **European Bank for Reconstruction and Development:** The EBRD is the largest single institutional investor in the private sector in the Balkans and also mobilizes significant amounts of foreign direct investment beyond its own financing capabilities. As of December 31, 2001, the EBRD had invested over €1.6 billion ($1.58 billion) in Croatia, Macedonia, Yugoslavia, and Bosnia; Croatia has benefited the most, with a total EBRD commitment of over €900 million ($890 million), while Bosnia has lagged behind, attracting just over €200 million ($198 million) of EBRD investment. See http://www.ebrd.org.

- **Southeast Europe Enterprise Development:** SEED is a five-year, $33 million, multi-donor initiative of the International Finance Corporation (IFC), part of the World Bank Group. Donor countries for SEED include Austria, Canada, Greece, the Netherlands, Norway, Slovenia, Sweden, Switzerland, and the U.K. SEED is designed to strengthen small and medium-sized enterprises (SMEs) in Bosnia and Herzegovina, Albania, Yugoslavia, and Kosovo by providing pre- and post-investment services and capacity building programs to local SMEs directly and to other organizations that support them. For more information, see http://www.ifc.org/seed.

- **European Investment Bank:** In the Balkans, the EIB specializes in infrastructure financing, in particular the rehabilitation and reconstruction of roads, railways, and power installations. Until 2000, the EIB focused primarily on funding projects in Romania and Bulgaria; since then, it has begun operations in Bosnia and Croatia, and has committed approximately €140 million ($138 million) for financing the reconstruction of the Yugoslav transport infrastructure sector. The EIB is an institution of the European Union; for more information, see http://www.eib.org.

NONGOVERNMENTAL ORGANIZATIONS AND
GRANT-MAKING FOUNDATIONS

There is a strong international not-for-profit, nongovernmental presence in the Balkans, comprised of Western grant-making foundations or nongovernmental organizations engaged in democracy promotion, civil society development, and training activities. Local civil society organizations are beginning to take root in the Balkans; however, despite the infusion of external assistance, local capacity in the civil society sector remains mixed, and indigenous organizations are unable to match the resources and influence of Western organizations.

The situation in the Balkans has also attracted the attention of think tanks and advocacy organizations. Two organizations noted for their work in the region are: the *International Crisis Group*, a private, multinational organization committed to strengthening the capacity of the international community to anticipate, understand, and act to prevent and contain conflict, and which has published 54 country reports and one book-length report on the region since 2000 (http://www.crisisweb.org); and the *European Stability Initiative*, a nonprofit research and policy institute that offers in-depth analysis of the complex issues involved in promoting stability and prosperity in southeast Europe (http://www.esiweb.org).

Among the major grant-making or nongovernmental organizations involved in the region are:

- **Soros Foundations:** The Open Society Institute, initiated and supported by the Soros foundations, operates in Albania, Bosnia, Croatia, Macedonia, Montenegro, and Serbia. The focus of funding varies from country to country but commonly emphasizes culture, civil society, education, the media, and programs for women and youth. See http://www.soros.org/osi.html.

- **Charles Stewart Mott Foundation:** This U.S.-based foundation awards grants to NGOs throughout the Balkans, and is particularly interested in funding NGOs that aim to improve ethnic relations in their communities. See http://www.mott.org/index.asp.

- **Friedrich Ebert Stiftung:** This German foundation funds educational and scholarship programs in Albania and Macedonia; see http://www.fes.bg/index_e.html.

- **King Baudouin Foundation:** The Belgian King Baudouin Foundation funds civil society development programs throughout southeast Europe; for more information, see http://www.kbs-frb.be/code/home.cfm?lang=en.

- **Partners for Democratic Change:** Partners for Democratic Change is committed to advancing civil society development through the building of sustainable local capacity, and also interested in mediation and conflict management. Partners operates locally managed national centers that work within communities to facilitate consensus-building and dispute resolution; it has centers in Albania and Kosovo and a regional center in Budapest. See http://www.partners-intl.org/.

- **National Endowment for Democracy:** The NED is a private not-for-profit organization that aims to strengthen democratic institutions by making grants to indigenous pro-democracy groups. In the year 2000, the NED gave more than $2.4 million in grants to the region, with the bulk of the awards going to Serbia, Kosovo, and Bosnia. See http://www.ned.org/grants/grants.html.

- **National Democratic Institute:** The NDI is a nonprofit organization that provides practical assistance to civic and political leaders in order to advance democratic values, practices, and institutions. In the Balkans it is involved with political party development, civic education, political transparency, election monitoring, and civil society development, among other areas. The NDI is active in Albania, Bosnia, Croatia, Macedonia, Serbia, Montenegro, and Kosovo; see http://www.ndi.org.

- **American Bar Association's Central and East European Law Initiative:** CEELI is a public service project of the American Bar Association and focuses on developing the rule of law through support for the legal reform process in central and eastern Europe. CEELI makes available pro bono U.S. legal expertise and assistance to emerging democracies that are in the process of restructuring their laws or legal systems, and also provides training programs. It has offices in Albania, Bosnia, Croatia, Kosovo, Macedonia, Montenegro, and Serbia. For more information, see http://www.abanet.org/ceeli/home.html.

- **International Foundation for Election Systems:** The IFES provides professional advice and technical assistance for the democratization process, focusing particularly on the legal framework for elections, electoral administration, and civic education. It also serves as a clearinghouse on democratic development. The IFES operates in Kosovo, Serbia, Macedonia, and Bosnia; see http://www.ifes.org.

- **International Republican Institute:** The IRI is interested in democracy promotion and the strengthening of free markets and the rule of law in developing democracies. Its programs include campaign management, polling, parliamentary training, judicial reform, and election monitoring, and it is active in Macedonia, Croatia, Serbia, and Albania (its projects in Croatia, Serbia, and Albania are being funded by USAID). See http://www.iri.org.

In addition to grant-making foundations and democracy promotion organizations, an array of international and local NGOs is active in the region—either through their own offices or linked with local partners—and is focused on such issues as humanitarian relief, including the provision of medical services; the plight of refugees; poverty; hunger; the special needs of women and children; psychosocial services; and education. The number and activity level of organizations in the Balkans is ever-changing and therefore difficult to catalog; as a general rule, there is a sharp increase in both during or after a crisis (such as the Kosovo conflict in 1999), which steadily declines once the most vital needs are met. Two sources of information on the civil society sector in the region are the *International Council of Voluntary Agencies* (ICVA), which has offices in Sarajevo and Belgrade and publishes a directory of civil

society organizations active in the region (see http://www.
icva-bh.org/eng); and USAID, which releases an annual NGO
Sustainability Index (for the 2001 edition, see http://www.usaid.
gov/regions/europe_eurasia/dem_gov/ngoindex/2001/index.htm).
Various websites also have information on NGO activity in the
region; these include NGONet (http://www.ngonet.org), Action
without Borders (http://www.idealist.org), and InterAction
(http://www.interaction.org).

THE BUSINESS COMMUNITY

In order to ensure the success of the political and economic transformation in the Balkans, it is necessary for the countries to move
beyond a reliance on aid and development assistance and leverage the resources of private interests through foreign or domestic direct investment. There are signs that outside investors are
beginning to take an interest in the region; for example, Stet
Telecom (Italy) and Hellenic Telecommunications Organization
(Greece) both have significant stakes in Telekom Serbia, while Alca-
tel (France) has a contract to provide a new mobile phone network
for Kosovo. These investments are large-scale and less dependent
upon good operating conditions on the ground. Other prominent
companies that have investments in the region include McDon-
alds, which operates franchises in Croatia and Serbia; Siemens,
which manufactures radio and television transmitters in Serbia under
the name "VF-Tel Siemensova"; British American Tobacco;
Philip Morris; Colgate-Palmolive; Coca-Cola; DHL; Ericsson
Electronics, which has invested approximately $47 million in
Croatia; Interbrew; PricewaterhouseCoopers; Portland Cement;
Volkswagen, which operates a factory in Bosnia; and 3M. For some
of these companies, the investments represent no more than
toeholds—a testing of the waters. Foreign capital is also uneven-
ly distributed, with Croatia and, increasingly, Serbia attracting
the lion's share of investment. Nevertheless, the investment of
well-established foreign companies into the region should be
encouraged.

There are several good sources of information on the private sectors in the Balkans, particularly in Croatia and Serbia. It should be noted that many of these sites are designed to attract foreign investors and so may be guilty of somewhat overoptimistic presentations.

- **Yugoslav Chamber of Commerce:** This site details tenders and projects, has a searchable index of foreign and domestic companies registered in Yugoslavia (including Kosovo), and offers information on relevant legislation and procedures for investors. See http://www.pkj.co.yu/en/YCCI.htm.

- **Southeastern Europe Chambers of Commerce and Industry Net:** This site provides information on business opportunities, registered companies, tenders and projects, public mandates, and legislation for Bosnia, Croatia, Macedonia, Montenegro, Slovenia, and Serbia. It also has links to individual countries' chambers of commerce. See http://www.se-cci.net/index_local.htm.

- **Foreign Investment Promotion Agency (Bosnia and Herzegovina):** FIPA is a federal agency established by Bosnia's central government in 1999, with the goal of promoting foreign direct investment. It offers guides and support services for investors, information on privatization, and various links; it seems to function as a starting point for foreign investors, though they may find its views on the feasibility of investment in Bosnia overly optimistic. See http://www.fipa.gov.ba.

- **Association of Balkan Chambers:** The Association of Balkan Chambers offers country profiles, market research, and links to the national chambers of commerce in Belgrade, Skopje, and Tirana, among others. See http://www.abcinfos.com/Index.html.

- **Central and Eastern Europe Business Information Center:** CEEBIC, which operates under the auspices of the U.S. Department of Commerce, is designed to facilitate the expansion of American business into central and eastern Europe. This site is the U.S. government's clearinghouse for the most recent economic, commercial, and financial information on the countries of central and eastern Europe. It offers trade and investment leads, market research, export guides, country commercial guides, and various other resources aimed at U.S. exporters and investors. See http://www.mac.doc.gov/ceebic/.

APPENDIX F-1: ECONOMIC STATISTICS AND DEMOGRAPHICS

This information represents a comparative compilation of data from sources such as the IMF, the World Bank, the United Nations Economic Commission for Europe, UNMIK, and the Federal Statistical Office of Yugoslavia. Due to the lack of precise cross-regional data, the information is indicative of the general status of economies but is not a precise measurement of economic performance.

COUNTRY STATISTICS
Basic Comparative Data

COUNTRY	Albania	Bosnia and Herzegovina	Croatia	Macedonia	Yugoslavia (Serbia & Montenegro)	Kosovo
Population (2001)	3.4 million	4.3 million	4.4 million	2.1 million	10.6 million	1.9 million
Pop. growth rate (2001)	0.88%	1.38%	1.48%	0.43%	−0.27 %	N/A
GDP purchasing power parity (2001)	$4.1 billion	$4.5 billion	$20.3 billion	$3.4 billion	$10.8 billion	$1.4–$1.9 billion
GDP per capita purchasing power parity (2001)	$1,205	$1,100	$4,605	$1,620	$940	$700–$1,000
Unemployment rate (2000)	16% officially; may be as high as 25%	35%–40%	22%	32%	30%	51%
Exports (2001)	$250 million	$1 billion	$4.6 billion	$1.2 billion	$2 billion	$167 million
Imports (2001)	$1 billion	$3.1 billion	$9 billion	$1.6 billion	$4.8 billion	$1.9 billion
Debt—external (2001)	$1.1 billion	$2.7 billion	$11.1 billion	$1.4 billion	$11.9 billion	N/A

Albania

Population:	3.4 million (2001 est.)
Age structure: **(2001 est.)**	*0–14 years:* 29.53% (male 536,495; female 500,026)
	15–64 years: 63.48% (male 1,073,351; female 1,155,115)
	65 years and over: 6.99% (male 107,476; female 138,021)
Population Growth Rate:	0.88% (2001 est.)
Ethnic Groups:	Albanian 95%, Greek 3%, other (Vlach, Romany, Serb, Bulgarian) 2% (1989 est.)

> *Note: In 1989, other estimates of the Greek population ranged from 1% (official Albanian statistics) to 12% (from a Greek organization)*

Languages:	Albanian (Tosk is the official dialect), Greek
GDP:	Purchasing power parity, $4.1 billion (2001 est.)
GDP real growth rate:	7.5% (2001 est.)
GDP per capita:	Purchasing power parity, $1,205 (2001 est.)
Labor force:	1.692 million (including 352,000 emigrant workers and 261,000 domestically unemployed) (1994 est.)
Unemployment:	16% (2000 est.)

> *Note: Unofficial estimates range as high as 25%*

Industries:	Food processing, textiles and clothing, lumber, oil, cement, chemicals, mining, basic metals, hydropower
Exports:	$250 million (2001 est.)

Export commodities:	Textiles and footwear, asphalt, metals and metallic ores, crude oil, vegetables, fruits, tobacco
Export partners:	Italy 67%, Greece 15%, Germany 5%, Austria 2%, Macedonia 2%
Imports:	$1.0 billion (2000 est.)
Import commodities:	Machinery and equipment, foodstuffs, textiles, chemicals
Import partners:	Italy 37%, Greece 28%, Turkey 6%, Germany 6%, Bulgaria 3% (2000 est.)
External debt:	$1.1 billion (2001)

Bosnia and Herzegovina

Population:	4.3 million (2001 est.)
	Note: All data dealing with population are subject to considerable error because of dislocations caused by military action and ethnic cleansing
Age structure: **(2001 est.)**	*0–14 years:* 20.13% (male 405,713; female 383,850)
	15–64 years: 70.78% (male 1,422,796; female 1,353,410)
	65 years and over: 9.09% (male 150,802; female 205,634)
Population Growth Rate:	1.38% (2001 est.)
Ethnic Groups:	Bosniak 44%, Serb 31%, Croat 17%, Yugoslav 5.5%, other 2.5% (1991 est.)
	Note: "Bosniak" has replaced "Muslim" as an ethnic term in part to avoid confusion with the religious term Muslim—an adherent of Islam
Languages:	Bosnian, Croatian, Serbian

GDP:	Purchasing power parity, $4.5 billion (2001 est.)
GDP real growth rate:	8% (2001 est.)
GDP per capita:	Purchasing power parity, $1,100 (2001 est.)
Labor force:	1.026 million
Unemployment:	35%–40% (2000 est.)
Industries:	Steel, coal, iron ore, lead, zinc, manganese, bauxite, vehicle assembly, textiles, tobacco products, wooden furniture, tank and aircraft assembly, domestic appliances, oil refining
Exports:	$1.0 billion (2001 est.)
Export commodities:	N/A
Export partners:	Croatia, Switzerland, Italy, Germany
Imports:	$3.1 billion (2001 est.)
Import commodities:	N/A
Import partners:	Croatia, Slovenia, Italy, Germany
External debt:	$2.7 billion (2001)

Croatia

Population:	4.4 million (2001 est.)
Age structure: **(2001 est.)**	*0–14 years:* 18.16% (male 403,722; female 383,151)
	15–64 years: 66.61% (male 1,452,872; female 1,434,086)
	65 years and over: 15.23% (male 245,727; female 414,584)
Population Growth Rate:	1.48% (2001 est.)
Ethnic Groups:	Croat 78.1%, Serb 12.2%, Bosniak 0.9%, Hungarian 0.5%, Slovenian 0.5%, Czech 0.4%, Albanian 0.3%, Montenegrin 0.3%, Roma 0.2%, other 6.6% (1991 est.)
Languages:	Croatian

GDP:	Purchasing power parity, $20.3 billion (2001 est.)
GDP real growth rate:	3.2% (2000 est.)
GDP per capita:	Purchasing power parity, $4,605 (2001 est.)
Labor force:	1.68 million (2000 est.)
Unemployment:	22% (2000 est.)
Industries:	Tourism, chemicals and plastics, machine tools, fabricated metal, electronics, pig iron and rolled steel products, aluminum, paper, wood products, construction materials, textiles, shipbuilding, petroleum and petroleum refining, food and beverages
Exports:	$4.6 billion (2001 est.)
Export commodities:	Transport equipment, textiles, chemicals, foodstuffs, fuels
Export partners:	Italy 18%, Germany 15.7%, Bosnia and Herzegovina 12.8%, Slovenia 10.6%, Austria 6.2%
Imports:	$9 billion (2001 est.)
Import commodities:	Machinery, transport and electrical equipment, chemicals, fuels and lubricants, foodstuffs
Import partners:	Germany 18.5%, Italy 15.9%, Russia 8.6%, Slovenia 7.9%, Austria 7.1% (1999 est.)
External debt:	$11.1 billion (2001)

Macedonia

Population:	2.1 million (2001 est.)
Age structure:	*0–14 years:* 22.92% (male 243,715; female 225,349)
(2001 est.)	*15–64 years:* 66.94% (male 688,484; female 681,225)

65 years and over: 10.14% (male 92,043; female 115,393)

Population Growth Rate:	0.43% (2001 est.)
Ethnic Groups:	Macedonian 66.6%, Albanian 22.7%, Turkish 4%, Roma 2.2%, Serb 2.1%, other 2.4% (1994 est.)
Languages:	Macedonian 70%, Albanian 21%, Turkish 3%, Serbo-Croatian 3%, other 3%
GDP:	Purchasing power parity, $3.4 billion (2001 est.)
GDP real growth rate:	5% (2000 est.)
GDP per capita:	Purchasing power parity, $1,620 (2000 est.)
Labor force:	1.0 million (1999 est.)
Unemployment:	32% (2000 est.)
Industries:	Coal, metallic chromium, lead, zinc, ferronickel, textiles, wood products, tobacco
Exports:	$1.2 billion (2001 est.)
Export commodities:	Food, beverages, tobacco, miscellaneous manufactures, iron and steel
Export partners:	Germany 22%, Yugoslavia 22%, U.S. 12%, Greece 7%, Italy 6% (2000 est.)
Imports:	$1.6 billion (2001 est.)
Import commodities:	Machinery and equipment, chemicals, fuels, food products
Import partners:	Germany 13%, Ukraine 13%, Russia 10%, Yugoslavia 8%, Greece 8% (2000 est.)
External debt:	$1.4 billion (2001)

Serbia and Montenegro

Population:	10.6 million (2001 est.) Serbia: 9,980,000 (2000 est.) Montenegro: 620,000 (2000 est.)

Age structure: **(2001 est.)**	*0–14 years:* 19.8% (male 1,095,905; female 1,024,123) *15–64 years:* 65.3% (male 3,415,728; female 3,553,343) *65 years and over:* 14.9% (male 681,559; female 906,632)
Population Growth Rate:	−0.27% (2001 est.)
Ethnic Groups:	Serb 62.6%, Albanian 16.5%, Montenegrin 5%, Hungarian 3.3%, other 12.6% (1991 est.)
Languages:	Serbian 95%, Albanian 5%
GDP:	Purchasing power parity, $10.8 billion (2001 est.)
GDP real growth rate:	15% (2000 est.)
GDP per capita:	Purchasing power parity, $940 (2001 est.)
Labor force:	1.6 million (1999 est.)
Unemployment:	30% (2000 est.)
Industries:	Machine building (aircraft, trucks, automobiles, tanks, weapons, electrical equipment, agricultural machinery), metallurgy (steel, aluminum, copper, lead, zinc, chromium, antimony, bismuth, cadmium), mining (coal, bauxite, nonferrous ore, iron ore, limestone), consumer goods (textiles, footwear, foodstuffs, appliances), electronics, petroleum products, chemicals, pharmaceuticals
Exports:	$2.0 billion (2001 est.)
Export commodities:	Manufactured goods, food and live animals, raw materials
Export partners:	Bosnia and Herzegovina, Italy, Macedonia, Germany (1998 est.)
Imports:	$4.8 billion (2001 est.)

Import commodities:	Machinery and transport equipment, fuels and lubricants, manufactured goods, chemicals, food and live animals, raw materials
Import partners:	Germany, Italy, Russia, Macedonia (1998 est.)
External debt:	$11.9 billion (2001)

Kosovo

Population:	1.9 million (2001)
Total fertility rate:	3.2 births per 1,000
Ethnic groups:	Albanian 90%, Serb 10%
GDP:	$1.4–$1.9 billion (2001)
GDP per capita:	$700–$1,000 (2001)
Unemployment rate:	51% (2000)
Natural resources:	Lead, zinc, nickel, coal, magnesium, lignite, kaolin, quartz, asbestos, limestone, marble, chrome, bauxite
Exports:	$167 million (2001)
Imports:	$1.9 billion (2001)

APPENDIX G: ACRONYMS AND ABBREVIATIONS

ANEM—The Association of Independent Electronic Media
BiH—Bosnia and Herzegovina (Bosni i Hercegovini)
CARDS—Community Assistance for Reconstruction, Development, and Stabilization
CEEBIC—Central and Eastern Europe Business Information Center
CEELI—American Bar Association's Central and Eastern European Law Initiative
CESID— Center for Free Elections and Democracy (Belgrade)
CJAU—Criminal Justice Advisory Unit (Bosnia)
COE—Council of Europe
CPA—Center for Preventive Action
DOS—Democratic Opposition of Serbia
EAR—European Agency for Reconstruction
EBRD—European Bank for Reconstruction and Development
EC—European Commission
ECHO—European Community Humanitarian Office
EIB—European Investment Bank
EU—European Union
EUPM—European Union Police Mission
FBiH—Federation of Bosnia and Herzegovina
FIPA—Foreign Investment Promotion Agency (Bosnia)
FRY—Federal Republic of Yugoslavia
FYROM—Former Yugoslav Republic of Macedonia
HDZ—Croatian Democratic Party (Hrvatska Demokratska Zajednica)
HPD—Housing and Property Directorate (Kosovo)
ICTY—International Criminal Tribunal for the Former Yugoslavia
ICVA—International Council of Voluntary Agencies
IDPs—Internally Displaced Persons
IFC—International Finance Corporation
IFES—International Foundation for Election Systems

IFIs—International Financial Institutions
IHRLG—International Human Rights Law Group
IJC—Independent Judicial Commission
IMF—International Monetary Fund
IPTF—International Police Task Force (Bosnia)
IRI—International Republican Institute
JIU—Judicial Inspection Unit (Kosovo)
KFOR—Kosovo Force
KJPC—Kosovo Judicial and Prosecutorial Council
KLA—Kosovo Liberation Army
KPC—Kosovo Protection Corps
KPS—Kosovo Police Service
MAP—Membership Action Program (NATO)
MUP—Ministry of Interior (Serbia) (Ministarstvo Unutrasnjih
  Poslova)
NAC—North Atlantic Council (NATO)
NATO—North Atlantic Treaty Organization
NDI—National Democratic Institute
NED—National Endowment for Democracy
NGO—Nongovernmental Organization
OHR—Office of High Representative (Bosnia and Herzegovina)
OSCE—Organization for Security and Cooperation in Europe
OTPOR—youth movement (Serbia)
PFP—Partnership for Peace (NATO)
PISG—Provisional Institutions of Self-Government (Kosovo)
RS—Republika Srpska (Bosnia and Herzegovina)
SAA—Stabilization and Association Agreement (European
  Union)
SACEUR—Supreme Allied Commander, Europe
SAP—Stabilization and Association Process (European Union)
SDS—Serb Democratic Party (Srpska Demokratska Stranka)
SEED—Southeast Europe Enterprise Development
SFOR—Stabilization Force in Bosnia and Herzegovina (NATO)
SME—small and medium sized enterprise
UN—United Nations
UNDP—United Nations Development Programme
UNHCR—United Nations High Commissioner for Refugees

UNMIBH—United Nations Mission in Bosnia and Herze-
govina
UNMIK—United Nations Mission in Kosovo
UNSRSG—United Nations Special Representative of the
Secretary-General
USAID—United States Agency for International Development
USIP—United States Institute of Peace
VAT—value-added tax
VJ—Yugoslav Army
WTO—World Trade Organization

CPA MISSION STATEMENT

The end of the Cold War brought down a world of empires and unleashed a flood of deadly ethnic and civil conflicts; it also set aside major-power competition, thus creating the possibility of resolving these deadly local conflicts. The Center for Preventive Action (CPA), founded by the Council on Foreign Relations in 1994, exists to help turn those possibilities into realities by uniting the anti-conflict stakeholders and offering tangible, practical strategies for peace.

In the last decade, this task has proved more desirable than realizable. Yet failing to try to prevent future Rwandas, Bosnias, and East Timors would be a terrible defeat for the human spirit. Nor will it do simply to continue trying and failing. Failure to prevent these horrors will amplify the problems—refugees, starvation, disease, political instability, and declining respect for government—that already plague relations between nations and the daily lives of citizens in conflict-torn areas.

Here is how the center will try to prevent deadly conflict caused by civil and ethnic violence, and why we believe we can succeed:

First, we will carefully select countries or regions where prevention has a decent chance, either before killing escalates or in lulls before new explosions. The center's Conflict Assessment Forum will draw upon the good analysis that many organizations are already doing, using their early warning studies to select areas where the center can make a difference. We do not intend to waste time redoing already sound work about problems and prospects. Our focus will be to forge agreement on where the center can be most useful.

Second, we will establish independent preventive action commissions of Council members and other experts who understand the roles and views of the stakeholders—governments, international organizations, nongovernmental organizations, and the business community—in specific conflict situations. These task forces will develop the necessary strategies (precise recommendations combined with concrete rewards and punishments) that might induce key leaders among the warring factions to see new self-interests in altering their behavior.

A critical mass of experts will be gathered to pool their knowledge, contacts, and influence; nothing less can succeed. The strategies developed will consist not simply of moralizing "oughts," "shoulds," and "musts"; they will provide realistic road maps with the incentives that will have the impact to change how leaders define their interests.

Third, we will comprehensively follow through in every way: prompting congressional hearings, writing op-eds, bringing the appropriate stakeholders, both local and international, together in private meetings, and more. The key here is to persevere, and to convince those who can take action that it can be successful—that the strategies offered by the center can work, or that the recommended plans can be readily reshaped by the actors to make them work.

These plans, no matter how persuasive, will fall on deaf ears unless the center can help improve public and governmental reception to conflict prevention. We will have to persuade leaders and citizens that prevention can be an effective and attainable instrument of U.S. foreign policy. This means doing studies, singly or with others, about the role of the military and its relationship with other government agencies and nongovernmental organizations. It means talking with legislators about how to meet their concerns regarding open-ended commitments and costs. It means strengthening international organizations. It means showing the business and financial worlds that they have an interest in peace, and that they can play a constructive role in conflict prevention.

CPA ADVISORY COMMITTEE